Pocket Rough Guide

Florence

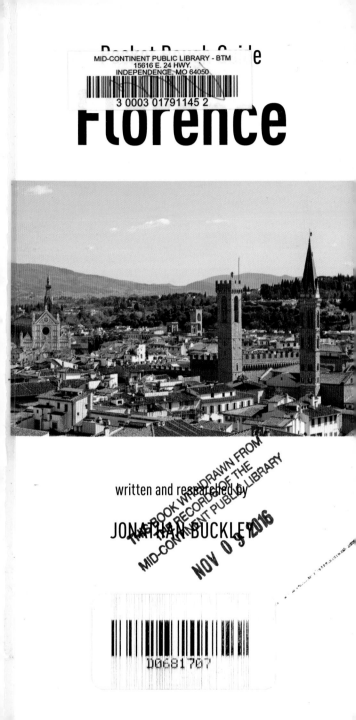

written and researched by

JONATHAN BUCKLEY

MID-CONTINENT PUBLIC LIBRARY - BTM
15616 E. 24 HWY.
INDEPENDENCE, MO 64050

3 0003 01791145 2

THIS BOOK WITHDRAWN FROM
THE RECORDS OF THE
MID-CONTINENT PUBLIC LIBRARY

NOV 03 2016

D0681707

Contents

INTRODUCTION TO

Florence

If one city could be said to encapsulate the essence of Italy it might well be Florence (Firenze in Italian), the first capital of the united country. The modern Italian language evolved from Tuscan dialect, and Dante's *Divina Commedia* was the first great work of Italian literature to be written in the vernacular; but what makes this city pivotal to the culture not just of Italy but of all Europe is, of course, the Renaissance. The very name by which we refer to this extraordinary era was coined by a Tuscan, Giorgio Vasari, who wrote in the sixteenth century of the "rebirth" of the arts with the humanism of Giotto and his successors. Every eminent artistic figure from Giotto onwards – Masaccio, Donatello, Botticelli, Leonardo da Vinci, Michelangelo – is represented here, in an unrivalled concentration of churches, galleries and museums.

PONTE VECCHIO AT DUSK

THE VIEW FROM PIAZZALE MICHELANGELO

Best spots for an al fresco meal or drink

Space is at a premium in central Florence, but across the river in Oltrarno there are plenty of places where you can eat and drink in the open air. On Piazza Santo Spirito several bars and restaurants have tables out on the square, while over on the east side of Oltrarno, the terraces of *Zoe* (p.120) and *Negroni* (p.119) – two of the city's most popular bars – are always buzzing.

During the fifteenth century, architects such as Brunelleschi and Alberti began to transform the cityscape of Florence, raising buildings that were to provide future generations with examples from which to take a lead. As soon as you step out of the train station the imprint of the Renaissance is visible, with the pinnacle of Brunelleschi's stupendous dome visible over the rooftops, and the Renaissance emphasis on harmony is exemplified with unrivalled eloquence in Brunelleschi's interiors of **San Lorenzo**, **Santo Spirito** and the **Cappella dei Pazzi**, and in Alberti's work at Santa Maria Novella and the Palazzo Rucellai. In painting, the development of the new sensibility can be plotted stage by stage in the vast picture collection of the recently expanded **Uffizi**, while the **Bargello**, the **Museo dell'Opera del Duomo** and the mighty guild church of **Orsanmichele** do the same for the story of sculpture. Equally revelatory are the fabulously decorated chapels of **Santa Croce** and **Santa Maria Novella**, forerunners of such astonishing creations as Masaccio's frescoes at **Santa Maria del Carmine**, Fra' Angelico's serene paintings at **San Marco**, and Andrea del Sarto's work at **Santissima Annunziata**, to name just a few. Florence is the city of Michelangelo, one of the dominant creative figures of sixteenth-century Italy, the scope of whose genius can only be appreciated after you've seen his astonishing San Lorenzo's **Sagrestia Nuova** and the marble statuary of the **Accademia** – home of the *David*. Michelangelo's two great rivals, Raphael and Titian, along with dozens of other supreme painters, are on show in the enormous art gallery of the **Palazzo Pitti,** once the home of the city's most famous family, the Medici, whose former home – the beautiful **Palazzo Medici-Riccardi** – can also be visited.

The achievements of the Renaissance were of course underpinned by the wealth that had been accumulated in earlier decades by the Medici and Florence's other plutocratic dynasties, and in every quarter of the centre you'll see churches and monuments that attest to the financial might of medieval Florence: the Duomo, the Baptistery, the Palazzo Vecchio, the huge churches of Santa Croce and Santa Maria Novella, and the exquisite Romanesque gem of San Miniato al Monte are among the most conspicuous demonstrations of Florence's prosperity. As for the centuries that followed the heyday of the Renaissance, it's often forgotten that Florence played a major role in the development of modern science – this was, after all, the home of **Galileo**, whose name has been bestowed on the city's fascinating science museum.

SAN LORENZO FOOD MARKET

It has to be said that nowadays it can often seem that Florence has become too popular for its own good. The city has been a magnet for tourists since the nineteenth century, when Stendhal staggered around its streets in a stupor of aesthetic delight, and nowadays, in high season, parts of the city can be almost unbearable, with immense queues for the Uffizi and pedestrian traffic at a standstill on the Ponte Vecchio. But if you time your visit carefully, don't rush around trying to see everything and make a point of eating and drinking in our recommended restaurants, cafés and bars, you'll have a visit you'll never forget.

When to visit

Midsummer in Florence can be less than pleasant: the heat is often stifling, and the inundation of tourists makes the major attractions a purgatorial experience. For the most enjoyable visit, arrive shortly before **Easter** or in **October**: the weather should be fine, and the balance between Florentines and outsiders restored to its rightful level. Winter is often quite rainy, but the absence of crowds makes this a good option for the big sights. If you can only travel between Easter and September, reserve your accommodation well before you arrive, as it's not uncommon for every hotel in the centre to be fully booked. The worst month is **August**, when the majority of Italians take their holidays, with the result that many restaurants and bars are closed for the month.

FLORENCE AT A GLANCE

>> EATING

As you'd expect in a major tourist city, Florence has plenty of restaurants, but – unsurprisingly – a large number of them are aimed squarely at the outsiders, so standards are often patchy, especially in the environs of Piazza della Signoria and Piazza del Duomo. But several good-quality and good-value restaurants lie on the periphery of the city centre, notably around **Santa Croce** and **Sant'Ambrogio**, and across the river in **Oltrarno**. Bear in mind also that simple meals are served in many Florentine bars and cafés, so if you fancy a quick bite to eat rather than a full-blown restaurant meal, take a look at our list of cafés and bars in each Places chapter of this guide.

>> DRINKING AND NIGHTLIFE

As elsewhere in Italy, the distinction between Florentine bars and cafés can be tricky to the point of impossibility, as almost every café serves alcohol and almost every bar serves coffee. That said, there are some cafés in which the emphasis is on coffee and cakes, just as there are plenty of bars dedicated to the **wines** of the Tuscan vineyards. The humblest wine bars belong to the endangered species known as the **vinaio**, which consists of little more than a few shelves of workaday wines plus a counter of snacks. At the opposite pole there's the **enoteca**, a place that has a vast wine menu and – usually – a good kitchen too.

Many of Florence's hotter bars try to keep the punters on the premises by serving free snacks with the **aperitivi** (usually about 7–9pm) before the music kicks in – either live or (more often) supplied by a DJ. Florence is quite a sedate city, but like every university town it has some decent clubs and music venues. For up-to-the-minute **information** about what's on, pick up a copy of *Firenze Spettacolo* or call in at Box Office, near the Sant'Ambrogio market at Via Delle Vecchie Carcere 1 (Mon–Fri 9.30am–7pm, Sat 9.30am–2pm; ⓦ boxofficetoscana.it) – it sells tickets for most events. A great online info source is ⓦ nottefiorentina.it.

>> SHOPPING

Florence is known as a producer of **luxury items**, notably gold jewellery, high-quality leather goods, top-grade stationery and marbled paper. The whole Ponte Vecchio is crammed with goldsmiths, but the city's premier shopping thoroughfare is **Via de' Tornabuoni**, where you'll find the showrooms of Italy's top fashion designers: Prada, Gucci, Armani, Dolce & Gabbana are all here, as are the country's main outlets for the top three Florentine fashion houses – Pucci, Roberto Cavalli and Ferragamo. For cheap and cheerful stuff there's the plethora of stalls around San Lorenzo, while if you want everything under one roof, there's also a handful of good **department stores**.

OUR RECOMMENDATIONS FOR WHERE TO EAT, DRINK AND SHOP ARE LISTED AT THE END OF EACH CHAPTER.

Day One in Florence

1 The Uffizi > p.46. The Uffizi is the obvious first stop: a mind-blowing parade of masterpieces, and it now has a whole new floor of galleries. If you're going in high season, be sure to book your ticket in advance or you face interminable queues.

2 Santa Croce > p.93. The vast church of Santa Croce has amazing frescoes by Giotto and other masters, and the Pazzi Chapel is one of the finest pieces of Renaissance architecture in Italy.

Lunch in Sant'Ambrogio > Grab a bargain lunch in the market (p.99) – perhaps some salami, cheeses and biscotti – or drop in on Florence's best pizzeria (p.101).

3 Ponte Vecchio > p.104. Take the picturesque route over the river into the Oltrarno district.

4 Palazzo Pitti > p.106. You could spend all day in the Pitti, which has several museums under its roofs – the Palatina galleries are the absolute highlight, with wonderful paintings by Raphael, Titian and many others.

5 Cappella Brancacci > p.113. Masaccio's frescoes are epoch-defining creations. If you want to see them, try booking a ticket before you arrive.

Aperitivo at *Il Rifrullo* (p.118), then a spot of dinner at *Filipepe* (p.120), followed by a nightcap at *Zoe* (p.120).

Day Two in Florence

1 The Bargello > p.50. Get
a crash-course in Renaissance
sculpture: Michelangelo, Cellini,
Donatello, Verrocchio – they are
all here.

2 The Duomo > p.30. The dome
of the Duomo has become the city's
trademark. Climb to the summit for
an unforgettable panorama.

3 Museo dell'Opera del Duomo
> p.36. Michelangelo's harrowing
Pietà, a roomful of amazing
Donatellos, the *Doors of Paradise*,
and much more.

Lunch > *Yellow Bar*
(p.57). It may not look
enticing, but *Yellow Bar* is one of
the best places in the city for an
unpretentious meal.

**4 San Lorenzo and Medici
tombs** > p.74. There's yet more from
Michelangelo and Donatello at the
mausoleum of Florence's quasi-royal
family – and don't miss the amazing
library next door.

**5 Santa Maria Novella and its
museum** > p.66. Alberti's facade
makes Santa Maria Novella perhaps
the city's most handsome church,
and a cornucopia of memorable
art is to be found inside, including
an exquisite fresco cycle by
Ghirlandaio.

Aperitivo at *Art Bar* (p.72)
then cross the water for
an evening meal at the chic and
innovative *Io* (p.121), one of the
most interesting restaurants to have
opened in the city for years.

Quiet Florence

Florence is one of Europe's busiest tourist destinations, but it's possible to escape the crowds, even in the centre of town. These places are rarely busy, and in the low season you could have some of them to yourself.

1 Museo Galileo > p.48. Everybody knows about the art, but few visitors bother themselves with Florence's scientific heritage – this fascinating museum fills in the story.

2 Santi Apostoli > p.59. This beautiful and ancient church is the most tranquil building in central Florence.

3 Santa Trinita > p.62. One of the chapels here has a gorgeous cycle of frescoes by Ghirlandaio.

4 Ognissanti > p.70. It has a Giotto painting, a Botticelli and two works by Ghirlandaio, but Ognissanti is overlooked by the tour groups.

Lunch > Buy your supplies at an *alimentari*, and wander out to the Cascine park (p.124) for a picnic lunch.

5 Santo Spirito > p.112. Don't be deterred by the blank exterior – Brunelleschi's spacious and serene church is a marvel of Renaissance design.

6 Santa Felicita > p.105. Located just yards from the Ponte Vecchio, Santa Felicita demands a visit for Pontormo's extraordinary *Deposition*.

7 San Miniato al Monte > p.116. Climb the hill to visit this glorious Romanesque building, and to marvel at the view, which is especially memorable at dusk.

Evening in Oltrarno > p.118 When it comes to eating and drinking, you're spoilt for choice on Florence's south bank.

Shopping Florence

The home town of Gucci, Pucci and Ferragamo has plenty of outlets that cater for gold-card holders, as you'd expect, but there are also some places to tempt those on less exalted budgets.

1 Coin and Rinascente > p.55 & p.39. Explore the city's two major department stores, finishing with a coffee on the roof of Rinascente.

2 San Lorenzo market > p.90. The avenues of market stalls at San Lorenzo will keep you browsing for the rest of the morning – and the food hall is irresistible.

Lunch > *Da Mario* (p.91), located just yards from the market hall, is a real Florentine institution.

3 The Santa Maria Novella perfumery > p.71. Florence's most gorgeous (and aromatic) shop is worth a visit just to inhale the air. But buy a bar of soap, at least.

4 Via de' Tornabuoni > p.63. Even if you can't afford a Pucci frock, window-shopping is fun on the city's designer row.

5 Scuola del Cuoio > p.99. Leather is a real Florentine speciality. Cross town to check out the biggest outlet for well-made and well-priced bags and belts.

6 Mercato delle Pulci > p.99. Who knows what you'll unearth among the junk of Florence's flea market?

Evening around Santa Croce and Sant'Ambrogio > *Cibrèo* (p.101) is the best restaurant in this part of town.

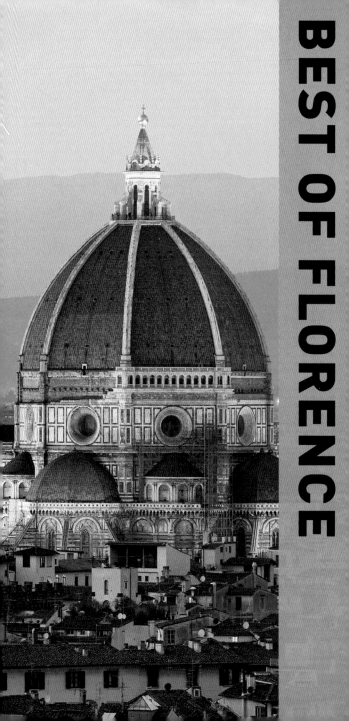

The museums

1 **The Museo dell'Opera del Duomo** Ghiberti's "Gates of Paradise" plus masterpieces by Donatello and Michelangelo are on show in this superb museum. **> p.36**

2 Palazzo Pitti The colossal Pitti palace contains a cluster of museums, one of them an amazing display of paintings. > **p.106**

4 The Uffizi The Medici art collection is simply the finest gathering of Italian Renaissance art on the planet. > **p.46**

3 The Accademia The home of Michelangelo's *David* draws enormous crowds – if you're visiting in summer, buy your ticket in advance. > **p.82**

5 The Bargello This stupendous museum of sculpture and applied arts is an essential complement to the Uffizi. > **p.50**

The churches

1 The Duomo Brunelleschi's magnificent dome, crowning the Duomo, is the city's defining image. > **p.30**

2 **Santa Maria Novella** Alberti's innovative facade fronts this art-packed church, featuring stunning frescoes by Uccello, Ghirlandaio, Masaccio and others. **> p.66**

3 **Santa Croce** Glorious frescoes by Giotto and the serene Pazzi chapel are but two of the treasures of the mighty Santa Croce. **> p.93**

4 **San Miniato al Monte** The resplendent San Miniato is a masterpiece of Romanesque architecture. **> p.116**

5 **San Lorenzo** The parish church of the Medici is also their mausoleum. **> p.74**

Frescoes

1 Palazzo Medici-Ricardi Glamorous portraits of some eminent members of the Medici clan can be seen in the exquisite little chapel of their family home. > **p.80**

2 San Marco An extraordinary sequence of frescoes by Fra' Angelico resides in the cells and chapels of the San Marco monastery. > **p.84**

3 The Cenacolo di Sant'Apollonia Depictions of the Last Supper were something of a Florentine speciality, and none is a more arresting vision of the event than Andrea del Castagno's. > **p.82**

4 Santa Maria del Carmine The startlingly original images created by Masaccio make the Carmine one of the most significant artistic monuments in Europe. > **p.113**

5 Santa Trinita Some of the Medici have walk-on roles in Ghirlandaio's scenes from the life of St Francis, in Santa Trìnita. > **p.62**

Bars and cafés

1 Gilli For a dose of bygone opulence, there's nowhere better than *Gilli*, a famous old café in the heart of the city. > **p.38**

2 Dolce Vita *Dolce Vita* has been a fixture of the Florentine night-life scene for a long time. **> p.118**

3 Le Volpi e L'Uve Fancy a snack and a reviving glass of Chianti after exploring the Pitti palace? The terrace of this well-run place is a perfect spot to linger. **> p.119**

4 Art Bar The homely *Art Bar* serves up some of the maddest cocktails in town. **> p.72**

5 Casa del Vino This busy little bar has a terrific selection of Tuscan wines. **> p.90**

21

Restaurants

1 Da Mario Unpretentious Tuscan cooking at honest prices has made *Da Mario* a longstanding lunchtime favourite. > **p.91**

2 Ora d'Aria High-class and imaginative cooking, just a few yards from the Uffizi. > **p.57**

3 Pane e Vino There are several good places to eat south of the river, and *Pane e Vino* is one of the best of them. > **p.122**

4 Cibrèo Some say it's become too popular for its own good, but nobody disputes the quality of the dishes at *Cibrèo*. > **p.101**

5 Enoteca Pinchiorri For that super-special occasion, nowhere beats the magnificent and hyper-expensive *Pinchiorri*. > **p.101**

Viewpoints

1 The Duomo Snap a fabulous cityscape from the summit of Brunelleschi's dome. > **p.30**

2 Ponte Santa Trìnita For the classic take on the Ponte Vecchio, walk downstream to Ponte Santa Trìnita. > **p.63**

3 The Campanile Not for the faint-hearted: it's a sheer 85-metre drop from the top of the bell-tower. > **p.32**

4 Piazzale Michelangelo Twenty minutes' walk from the river and you'll have the entire city centre laid out before you. > **p.115**

5 Fiesole To get the whole of Florence in the frame, take the bus up to Fiesole. > **p.128**

Michelangelo

1 The Pietà Michelangelo depicts himself in one of his last works, the Museo dell'Opera del Duomo's *Pietà*. > **p.36**

2 **The Biblioteca Medicea-Laurenziana** The bizarre vestibule and the well-ordered reading room of the Laurentian Library were both designed by Michelangelo. > **p.78**

3 **Brutus** The redoubtable *Brutus* shares a room with other masterpieces by Michelangelo. > **p.50**

4 **The Santo Spirito Crucifix** The Crucifix in the sacristy of Santo Spirito is generally agreed to be a youthful work by Michelangelo. > **p.112**

5 **The Medici tombs** These monuments – carved by Michelangelo, set in a chapel designed by him – are every bit as enthralling as the *David*. > **p.79**

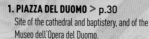

PLACES

1. PIAZZA DEL DUOMO > p.30
Site of the cathedral and baptistery, and of the Museo dell'Opera del Duomo.

2. PIAZZA DELLA SIGNORIA > p.40
The political centre of Florence, dominated by the Palazzo Vecchio. The Uffizi gallery is right next door.

3. WEST OF THE CENTRE > p.58
Florence's smartest shops are found immediately west of the Piazza della Signoria; beyond them, the area's major monument is Santa Maria Novella.

4. NORTH OF THE CENTRE > p.74
The Medici church of San Lorenzo, on the edge of the city's main market, is one of the focal points to the north, along with the Accademia, San Marco and Santissima Annunziata.

5. EAST OF THE CENTRE > p.92
To the east of the centre, all roads lead to gargantuan church of Santa Croce; it's also a great district for foodies and has some lively bars.

6. OLTRARNO > p.104
Florence's south bank is centred on the stupendous Palazzo Pitti, with the city's finest garden out the back. After dark, this is where much of the action is.

7. THE OUTSKIRTS > p.124
The biggest park is on the very periphery of the centre, as is the home of Florence's famous football team.

8. FIESOLE > p.128
Perched on a hill to the north of the city, the village of Fiesole is a pleasant spot to cool down and get away from the crowds.

Piazza del Duomo and around

All first-time visitors gravitate towards Piazza del Duomo, beckoned by the pinnacle of Brunelleschi's dome, which lords it over the cityscape with an authority unmatched by any architectural creation in any other Italian city. Yet even though the magnitude of the Duomo is apparent from a distance, the first sight of the cathedral and the adjacent Baptistery still comes as a jolt, their colourful patterned exteriors making a startling contrast with the dun-toned buildings around.

Once you've finished exploring these mighty monuments, the obvious next step is to visit the superb Museo dell'Opera del Duomo, a vast repository for works of art removed over the centuries from the Duomo, Baptistery and Campanile.

THE DUOMO

Piazza del Duomo Ⓦ operaduomo.firenze.it.
Mon–Wed & Fri 10am–5pm, Thurs
10am–4.30pm (4pm in May & Oct, 5pm July–Sept), Sat 10am–4.45pm, Sun 1.30–4.45pm.
Free. MAP P.32, POCKET MAP C10–D10

Some time in the seventh century the seat of the Bishop of Florence was transferred from San Lorenzo to Santa Reparata, a sixth-century church which stood on the site

of the present-day Duomo, or **Santa Maria del Fiore** to give it its full name. Later generations modified this older church until 1294, when Arnolfo di Cambio drafted a scheme to create the largest church in the Catholic world. Progress on the project faltered after Arnolfo's death in 1302, but by 1418 only the dome – no small matter – remained unfinished.

Tickets for the Piazza del Duomo sights

In addition to tickets for single admission, you can buy an €11 ticket for the Dome plus the Museo dell'Opera, a €15 ticket for the Campanile, Santa Reparata, Baptistery and Museo, and a €23 ticket for all five. These tickets are valid for four days, and can be bought at any of these sights.

Parts of the Duomo's **exterior** date back to Arnolfo's era, but most of the overblown main facade is a nineteenth-century pseudo-Gothic front. The most attractive external adornment is the **Porta della Mandorla** on the north side. This doorway takes its name from the almond-shaped frame (or *mandorla*) that contains *The Assumption of the Virgin* (1414–21), sculpted by Nanni di Banco.

The Duomo's **interior** is a vast, uncluttered enclosure of bare masonry, alleviated by a pair of frescoed memorials to *condottieri* (mercenary commanders) on the north side of the nave: Paolo Uccello's monument to Sir John Hawkwood, created in 1436, and Andrea del Castagno's monument to Niccolò da Tolentino, painted twenty years later. Just beyond the horsemen, Domenico di Michelino's 1465 *Dante Explaining the Divine Comedy* gives Brunelleschi's dome – then nearing completion – a place only marginally less prominent than the mountain of Purgatory.

Barriers usually prevent visitors from going any further, but you might be able to take a look into the **Sagrestia Nuova**, where the lavish panelling is inlaid with beautiful intarsia work (1436–45) by Benedetto and Giuliano Maiano. The mighty sacristy door (1445–69),

created in conjunction with Michelozzo, was Luca della Robbia's only work in bronze. It was in this sacristy that Lorenzo de' Medici took refuge in 1478 after his brother Giuliano had been mortally stabbed on the altar steps by the Pazzi conspirators (see box, p.34); the bulk of the recently installed doors protected him from his would-be assassins. Small portraits on the handles commemorate the brothers.

In the 1960s, remnants of the Duomo's predecessor, **Santa Reparata** (same hours as Duomo, except closed Sun; €3), were uncovered underneath the west end of the nave. Subsequent diggings have revealed a complicated jigsaw of Roman, Paleochristian and Romanesque remains, plus fragments of mosaic and fourteenth-century frescoes and Brunelleschi's tomb, a marble slab so unassuming that it had lain forgotten under the south aisle.

Climbing the **dome** (Mon–Fri 8.30am–7pm, Sat 8.30am–5.40pm; €8) is an amazing experience, both for the views from the top and for the insights it offers into Brunelleschi's engineering genius (see box, p.33). Be prepared to queue, and be ready for the 463 lung-busting steps. Claustrophobics should note that the climb involves some very confined spaces.

31

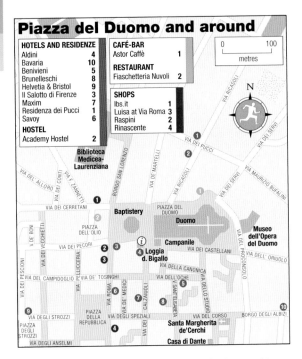

Piazza del Duomo and around

HOTELS AND RESIDENZE	
Aldini	4
Bavaria	10
Benivieni	5
Brunelleschi	8
Helvetia & Bristol	9
Il Salotto di Firenze	3
Maxim	7
Residenza dei Pucci	1
Savoy	6

HOSTEL	
Academy Hostel	2

CAFÉ-BAR	
Astor Caffè	1

RESTAURANT	
Fiaschetteria Nuvoli	2

SHOPS	
Ibs.it	1
Luisa at Via Roma	3
Raspini	2
Rinascente	4

THE CAMPANILE

Piazza del Duomo ⓦ operaduomo.firenze.it.
Daily 8.30am–7.30pm. €6. MAP P.32,
POCKET MAP C10

The Campanile was begun in
1334 by Giotto during his

period as official city architect
and *capo maestro* (head of
works) in charge of the
Duomo. By the time of his
death three years later, the
base, the first of five eventual
levels, had been completed.
Andrea Pisano, fresh from
creating the Baptistery's south
doors (see p.34), continued
construction of the second
storey (1337–42), probably in
accordance with Giotto's plans.
Work was rounded off by
Francesco Talenti, who
rectified deficiencies in Giotto's
original calculations in the
process: the base's original
walls teetered on the brink of
collapse until he doubled their
thickness. When completed,
the bell tower reached 84.7m,
well over the limit set by the
city in 1324 for civic towers.

The tower's decorative
sculptures and reliefs – they

are copies; the originals are in the Museo dell'Opera del Duomo (see p.37) – illustrate humanity's progress from original sin to a state of divine grace, a progress facilitated by manual labour, the arts and the sacraments, and guided by the influence of the planets and the cardinal and theological virtues.

A climb to the summit is one of the highlights of any Florentine trip: the parapet at the top of the tower is a less lofty but in many ways more satisfying viewpoint than the cathedral dome, if only because the view takes in the dome itself. There are 414 steps to the summit – and there's no lift.

THE DUOMO'S DOME

Brunelleschi's dome

Since Arnolfo di Cambio's scale model of the Duomo collapsed some time in the fourteenth century, nobody has been sure quite how he intended to crown his achievement. In 1367 Neri di Fioraventi proposed the construction of a magnificent cupola that was to span nearly 43m, broader than the dome of Rome's Pantheon, which had been the world's largest for 1300 years.

There was just one problem: nobody had worked out how to build such a thing. Medieval arches were usually built on wooden "centring", a network of timbers that held the stone in place until the mortar was set. In the case of the Duomo, the weight of the stone would have been too great for the timber. Eventually the project was thrown open to competition, and a goldsmith and clockmaker, Filippo Brunelleschi, presented the winning scheme. The key to Brunelleschi's success lay in the construction of the dome as two masonry shells, each built as a stack of ever-diminishing rings. Secured with hidden stone beams and enormous iron chains, these concentric circles formed a lattice that was filled with lightweight bricks laid in a herringbone pattern that prevented the higher sections from falling inwards.

The dome's completion was marked by the consecration of the cathedral on March 25, 1436 – Annunciation Day, and the Florentine New Year – in a ceremony conducted by the pope. Even then, the topmost piece, the lantern, remained unfinished, with many people convinced the dome could support no further weight. But once again Brunelleschi won the day, beginning work on the dome's final stage in 1446, just a few months before his death. The whole thing was finally completed in the late 1460s, when the cross and gilded ball, both cast by Verrocchio, were hoisted into place. It is still the largest masonry dome in the world.

THE BAPTISTERY

Piazza del Duomo ⓦ operaduomo.firenze.it.
Mon–Sat 11.15am–7pm, Sun & first Sat of
month 8.30am–2pm. €5. MAP P.32.
POCKET MAP C10

Generally thought to date from
the sixth or seventh century,
the Baptistery is the **oldest
building** in Florence, and was
first documented in 897, when
it was the city's cathedral.

The Florentines were always
conscious of their Roman
ancestry, and for centuries
believed that the Baptistery was
a converted Roman temple to
Mars. This isn't the case, but its
exterior marble cladding –
applied between about 1059
and 1128 – is clearly classical in
inspiration, while its most
famous embellishments, the
gilded **bronze doors**, mark the
emergence of a more scholarly,
self-conscious interest in the
art of the ancient world.

The arrival of Andrea Pisano
in Florence in 1330 offered the
chance to outdo the celebrated
bronze portals of archrival
Pisa's cathedral. Most of the
south doors' 28 panels,
installed in 1339, form a
narrative on the life of St John
the Baptist, patron saint of
Florence and the Baptistery's
dedicatee.

Some sixty years of financial
and political turmoil, and the
ravages of the Black Death,
prevented further work on the
Baptistery's other entrances
until 1401. That year a

The Pazzi Conspiracy

The Pazzi Conspiracy had its roots in the election in 1472 of Pope Sixtus
IV, who promptly made six of his nephews cardinals. One of them,
Girolamo Riario, received particularly preferential treatment, probably
because he was in fact Sixtus's son. Sixtus's plan was that Riario should
take over the town of Imola as a base for papal expansion, and accordingly
he approached Lorenzo de' Medici for the necessary loan. When Lorenzo
rebuffed him, and in addition refused to recognize Francesco Salviati as
archbishop of Pisa, a furious Sixtus turned to the Pazzi, the Medici's leading
Florentine rivals as bankers in Rome.

Three co-conspirators met in Rome in the early months of 1477: Riario,
now in possession of Imola but eager for greater spoils; Salviati,
incandescent at Lorenzo's veto; and Francesco de' Pazzi, head of the Pazzi's
Rome operation and determined to usurp Medici power in Florence. After
numerous false starts, it was decided to murder Lorenzo and Giuliano while
they attended Mass in Florence's cathedral. The date set was Sunday, April
26, 1478: Lorenzo's extermination was delegated to two embittered priests,
Maffei and Bagnone, whereas Giuliano was to be dispatched by Francesco
de' Pazzi and Bernardo Baroncelli, a Pazzi sidekick.

It all went horribly wrong. Giuliano was killed, but Lorenzo managed to
escape, fleeing wounded to the Duomo's new sacristy. The conspirators
were soon dealt with: Salviati and Francesco de' Pazzi were hanged from a
window of the Palazzo della Signoria; Maffei and Bagnone were castrated
and hanged; Baroncelli escaped to Constantinople but was extradited and
executed; and Jacopo de' Pazzi, the godfather of the Pazzi clan, was
tortured, hanged alongside the decomposing Salviati and finally hurled
into the river.

competition was held to design a new set of doors, with the entrants being asked to create a panel showing the Sacrifice of Isaac. The judges found themselves equally impressed by the work of two young goldsmiths, **Brunelleschi** and **Lorenzo Ghiberti**; both winning entries are displayed in the Bargello (see p.50). Unable to choose between the pair, the judges suggested that they work in tandem. Brunelleschi replied that if he couldn't do the job alone he wasn't interested – whereupon the contract was handed to Ghiberti.

His **north doors** (1403–24) show a new naturalism and classicized sense of composition, but they are as nothing to the gilded **east doors** (1425–52), which have long been known as the "Gates of Paradise", supposedly because Michelangelo once remarked that they were so beautiful they deserved to be the portals of heaven. These are copies – the originals are in the Museo dell'Opera del Duomo (see p.36).

The Baptistery **interior** is stunning, with its black and white marble cladding and miscellany of ancient columns below a blazing thirteenth-

THE BAPTISTERY

century mosaic ceiling, dominated by Christ in Judgement. The interior's semi-abstract mosaic pavement also dates from the thirteenth century. The empty octagon at its centre marks the spot once occupied by the huge font in which every child born in the city during the previous twelve months would be baptized on March 25 (New Year's Day in the old Florentine calendar). To the right of the altar lies the tomb of Baldassare Cossa, the schismatic Pope John XXIII, who was deposed in 1415 and died in Florence in 1419.

THE CEILING OF THE BAPTISTERY

THE MUSEO DELL'OPERA DEL DUOMO

Piazza del Duomo ⓦ operaduomo.firenze.it.
Mon–Sat 9am–7.30pm, Sun 9am–1.40pm. €6.
MAP P.32, POCKET MAP D10

In 1296 a body called the Opera del Duomo, literally the "Work of the Duomo", was created to oversee the maintenance of the Duomo. Since the early fifteenth century its home has been the building behind the east end of the cathedral at Piazza del Duomo 9, which now also houses the Museo dell'Opera del Duomo, a repository of the most precious and fragile works of art from the Duomo, Baptistery and Campanile. Work is now under way to double the exhibition space at this museum; the project is scheduled for completion in 2016, so for some time yet the layout should stay as it's described below.

Beyond the ticket office, rooms given over to Gothic sculpture from the Baptistery and the Duomo precede the museum's **courtyard**, now the

LUCA DELLA ROBBIA'S CANTORIA

home of all eight of Ghiberti's panels from the "Doors of Paradise", sharing the space with the graceful *Baptism of Christ* (1502–25), by Andrea Sansovino and assistants.

The largest room on this floor is devoted to the original sculptures of the cathedral's west front. Foremost among these are works by the cathedral's first architect, **Arnolfo di Cambio** (and his workshop), including an eerily glass-eyed *Madonna and Child* and the vase-carrying figure of *St Reparata*, one of Florence's patron saints.

Up the stairs on the mezzanine level stands **Michelangelo**'s anguished *Pietà* (1550–53), moved from the cathedral in 1981 while restoration of the dome was in progress. This is one of the sculptor's last works, carved when he was almost 80, and was intended for his own tomb; Vasari records that the face of Nicodemus is a self-portrait. Dissatisfied with the quality of the marble, Michelangelo mutilated the group by hammering off the left leg and arm of Christ; a pupil restored the arm, then finished off the figure of Mary Magdalene.

Although he's represented on the lower floor, it's upstairs that **Donatello**, the greatest of Michelangelo's precursors, really comes to the fore. The first room at the top of the stairs features his magnificent *Cantoria*, or choir loft (1433–39), with its playground of boisterous *putti*. Facing it is another splendid *cantoria* (1431–38), the first-known major commission of the young **Luca della Robbia** (the originals are underneath, with casts replacing them in the *cantoria* itself).

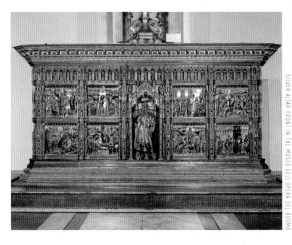

Around the room are arrayed the life-size figures that Donatello carved for the Campanile, perhaps the most powerful of which is the prophet Habakkuk, the intensity of whose gaze is said to have prompted the sculptor to seize it and yell, "Speak, speak!" Keeping company with Donatello's work are four Prophets (1348–50) and two Sibyls (1342–48) attributed to Andrea Pisano, and *The Sacrifice of Isaac* (1421), a collaboration between Nanni di Bartolo and Donatello.

Donatello's later style is exemplified by the gaunt wooden figure of Mary Magdalene (1453–55), which confronts you on entering the room off the *cantorie* room. The *Magdalene* came from the Baptistery, as did the silver altar-front at the far end of the room, a dazzling summary of the life of St John the Baptist. Begun in 1366, the piece was completed in 1480, the culmination of a century of labour by, among others, Michelozzo, Antonio del Pollaiuolo and Verrocchio.

On the other side of the *cantorie* room you'll find the bas-reliefs that once adorned the Campanile, depicting the spiritual refinement of humanity through labour, the arts and, ultimately, the virtues and sacraments. The display reproduces the reliefs' original arrangement, the key panels being the hexagonal reliefs of the lower tier, all of which – save for the last five, by Luca della Robbia (1437–39) – were the work of Andrea Pisano and his son Nino (c.1348–50), probably to designs by Giotto.

A corridor leads from here past a display of some of the tools used to build the Duomo's dome. Brunelleschi's death mask, at the angle of the corridor, precedes a sequence of rooms showing various proposals for the completion of the balcony of the drum below the cupola and the Duomo's facade. The wooden model of the cathedral lantern is presumed to have been made by Brunelleschi as part of his winning proposal for the design of the lantern in 1436.

Florence – the capital of Italy

At the start of 1865 Florence became the first capital of the newly united Italy. It was to hold this position for only five years, but during this period a transformation of the city was begun, following a plan conceived by Giuseppe Poggi (1811–1901). The city walls were demolished, and wide boulevards or *viali* put in their place; shopping streets such as Via de' Cerretani and Via de' Tornabuoni were widened and modernized; the riverbanks were developed; and Piazzale Michelangelo was created on the hill of San Miniato. But the most drastic intervention in the city centre was the removal of the old market and the surrounding slums – a new market hall was built near San Lorenzo, and the ancient market area became Piazza della Repubblica.

PIAZZA DELLA REPUBBLICA

MAP P.32, POCKET MAP B11

A short distance to the south of Piazza del Duomo, the vacant expanse of Piazza della Repubblica opens up. Impressive solely for its size, this square was planned in the late 1860s, as part of Giuseppe Poggi's masterplan for the capital of the recently formed Italian nation. However, the clearance of the **Mercato Vecchio** had not even begun when the capital was transferred to Rome, and it wasn't until 1885 that the marketplace and its disease-ridden tenements were finally swept away. On the west side a vast **arch** bears the triumphant inscription: "The ancient city centre restored to new life from the squalor of centuries."

The free standing column is the solitary trace of the piazza's history. Once surrounded by stalls, it used to be topped by Donatello's statue of Abundance, and a bell that was rung to signal the start and close of trading. Nowadays, Piazza della Repubblica is best known for the three large and expensive **cafés** that stand on the perimeter: the *Gilli*, the most attractive of the trio, founded way back in 1733 (albeit on a different site – it moved here in 1910); the *Giubbe Rosse*, once the intellectuals' café of choice (the Futurist manifesto was launched here in 1909); and the *Paszkowski*, which began business as a beer hall in the 1840s.

Shops

IBS.IT

Via de' Cerretani 16r ☎ 055 287 339, Ⓦ ibs.it.
Mon–Thurs 9am–8pm, Fri & Sat 9am–midnight,
Sun 10am–8pm. MAP P.32, POCKET MAP B10

Florence's branch of the
nationwide IBS is the biggest
bookshop in the city – only
neighbouring Feltrinelli has
anything like as much stock.

LUISA AT VIA ROMA

Via Roma 19–21r ☎ 055 217 826,
Ⓦ luisaviaroma.com. Mon–Sat 10am–7.30pm,
Sun 11am–7pm. MAP P.32, POCKET MAP B10

Luisa was founded back in the
1930s and remains Florence's
top-end multi-label clothes shop.
The interior is one of Florence's
more impressive examples of
modern architectural design.

RASPINI

Via Roma 25–29r ☎ 055 213 077 & Via Por
Santa Maria 70r ☎ 055 213 901, Ⓦ raspini
.com. Mon 3.30–7.30pm, Tues–Sat
10.30am–7.30pm, plus last Sun of month
10am–7pm. MAP P.32, POCKET MAP C10

Not quite as exclusive as the
nearby Luisa (see above), the
elegant Raspini always has a
good stock of clothes from a
range of designers, and is
usually strong on diffusion
lines. These are the two main
branches; leftovers from the
previous season are sold at big
discounts at Raspini Vintage,
Via Calimaruzza 17r, behind
the Via Por Santa Maria branch
(map p.42, Pocket map C12).

RINASCENTE

Piazza della Repubblica 1 ☎ 055 239 8544,
Ⓦ www.rinascente.it. Mon–Sat 9am–9pm, Sun
10.30am–8pm. MAP P.32, POCKET MAP C11

Like Coin (see p.55),
Rinascente is part of a
countrywide chain, though this
store, opened in 1996, is a
touch more upmarket than its
nearby rival, and bigger, with

CANTUCCI AT GILLI

six floors of clothes, linen,
cosmetics, and other household
stuff. The rooftop café gives a
great view of the Duomo.

Café-bar

ASTOR CAFFÈ

Piazza del Duomo 20r ☎ 055 239 9318,
Ⓦ astorcafe.com. Daily 9am–3am. MAP P.32,
POCKET MAP D10

This is the hottest spot on the
piazza, with a glitzy interior
spread over three floors. Up to
10pm it's a café-bar-grill, then
the DJs get to work, playing
anything from hip-hop to
Brazilian music, every night.

Restaurant

FIASCHETTERIA NUVOLI

Piazza dell'Olio 15 ☎ 055 239 6616. Mon–Sat
noon–9pm. MAP P.32, POCKET MAP B10

For a basic meal within a
stone's throw of the Duomo,
you can't do better than this.
Upstairs, the tiny, dark,
bottle-lined bar is dominated
by a counter laden with cold
meats, *crostini* and other
snacks. In the basement,
good-value Florentine staples
are served at half a dozen
communal tables.

Piazza della Signoria and around

Whereas the Piazza del Duomo provides the focus for the city's religious life, the Piazza della Signoria – site of the magnificent Palazzo Vecchio and forecourt to the Uffizi gallery – has always been the centre of its secular existence. Created in 1307, to provide a setting for the Palazzo Vecchio, the piazza was paved by 1385 and reached its present-day dimensions in 1871, after Florence's brief spell as the capital of the country.

The dense network of streets northeast of the Piazza della Signoria is dominated by the campanile of the Badìa Fiorentina, the most important of several buildings in the area that have the strongest associations with Dante Alighieri. Immediately opposite the church stands the forbidding bulk of the Bargello, once the city's prison, now home to a superb collection of sculpture and objets d'art. To the south of the Bargello, at the back of the Uffizi, lies the fascinating Museo Galileo, a sight too often overlooked by art-obsessed visitors.

The main catwalk of the Florentine *passeggiata* is Via dei Calzaiuoli, the broad avenue that links Piazza della Signoria with Piazza del Duomo. Shop-lined for most of its length, it boasts one stupendous monument, the church of Orsanmichele.

THE PIAZZA DELLA SIGNORIA STATUES

MAP P.42, POCKET MAP C12

Florence's political volatility is encapsulated by the Piazza della Signoria's array of **statues**. From left to right, the line-up starts with Giambologna's equestrian statue (1587–94) of Cosimo I; mimicking the famous Marcus Aurelius statue in Rome, it was designed to draw parallels between the power of medieval Florence (and thus Cosimo) and the glory of imperial Rome. Next comes Ammannati's fatuous **Neptune** fountain (1565–75), a tribute to Cosimo's prowess as a naval commander. Neptune himself is a lumpen lout of a figure, who provoked Michelangelo to coin the rhyming put-down *Ammannato, Ammannato, che bel marmo hai rovinato* ("…what a fine piece of marble you've ruined"). After a copy of Donatello's *Marzocco* (1418–20), the original of which is in the Bargello, comes a replica of the same sculptor's *Judith and Holofernes* (1456–60), which freezes the action at the moment Judith's arm begins its scything stroke – a dramatic conception that no

THE LOGGIA DELLA SIGNORIA

other sculptor of the period would have attempted. Commissioned by Cosimo de' Medici, this statue doubled as a fountain in the Palazzo Medici but was removed to the Piazza della Signoria after the expulsion of the family in 1495, to be displayed as an emblem of vanquished tyranny; the original is in the Palazzo Vecchio.

Michelangelo's **David**, at first intended for the Duomo, was also installed here in 1504 as a declaration of civic solidarity by the Florentine Republic; the original is now cooped up in the Accademia (see p.82). Bandinelli's adjacent *Hercules and Cacus* (1534) was designed as a personal emblem of Cosimo I and a symbol of Florentine fortitude. Benvenuto Cellini described the muscle-bound Hercules as looking like "a sackful of melons".

THE LOGGIA DELLA SIGNORIA

MAP P.42, POCKET MAP C12-C13

The square's grace note, the Loggia della Signoria, was completed in 1382 and served as a dais for city dignitaries, a forum for meeting foreign emissaries and a platform for the swearing-in of public officials. Its alternative name,

the Loggia dei Lanzi, comes from Cosimo I's bodyguard of Swiss lancers, who were garrisoned nearby.
Although Donatello's *Judith and Holofernes* was placed here as early as 1506, it was only in the late eighteenth century that the loggia became exclusively a **showcase** for sculpture. In the corner nearest the Palazzo Vecchio stands a figure that has become one of the iconic images of the Renaissance, Benvenuto Cellini's *Perseus* (1554). Made for Cosimo I, the statue symbolizes the triumph of firm grand ducal rule over the monstrous indiscipline of all other forms of government. Equally attention-seeking is Giambologna's last work, to the right, *The Rape of the Sabine* (1583), the epitome of the Mannerist obsession with spiralling forms. The sculptor intended the piece merely as a study of old age, male strength and female beauty; the present name was coined after the event. The figures along the back wall are Roman works, traditionally believed to portray empresses, while of the three central statues only one – Giambologna's *Hercules Slaying the Centaur* (1599) – deserves such prominence.

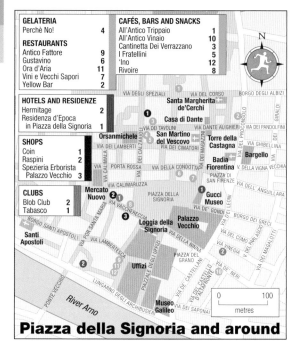

GELATERIA		CAFÉS, BARS AND SNACKS	
Perchè No!	4	All'Antico Trippaio	1
		All'Antico Vinaio	10
RESTAURANTS		Cantinetta Dei Verrazzano	3
Antico Fattore	9	I Fratellini	5
Gustavino	6	'Ino	12
Ora d'Aria	11	Rivoire	8
Vini e Vecchi Sapori	7		
Yellow Bar	2		

HOTELS AND RESIDENCE	
Hermitage	2
Residenza d'Epoca in Piazza della Signoria	1

SHOPS	
Coin	1
Raspini	2
Spezieria Erborista Palazzo Vecchio	3

CLUBS	
Blob Club	2
Tabasco	1

Piazza della Signoria and around

THE GUCCI MUSEO

Piazza della Signoria 10. Daily 10am–8pm.
€6. MAP P.42, POCKET MAP D12

The piazza's massive
fourteenth-century Palazzo
della Mercanzia now houses
the Gucci Museo, a temple to
Florence's most famous
fashion house. As you'd
expect, there are some
fabulous clothes here,
plus a plethora of ridiculous
items such as Gucci-
monogrammed scuba flippers.
Contemporary art from the
vast collection of François-
Henri Pinault, boss of the
company that owns Gucci, is
also on show; there's a
bookshop, café and gift shop
too, in case you want to drop
a couple of hundred euros on
a Gucci belt.

COSIMO I IN FRONT OF THE GUCCI MUSEO

The Florentine Republic

Between 1293 and 1534 – bar the odd ruction – Florence maintained a republican constitution that was embodied in well-defined institutions. The rulers were drawn from the ranks of guild members over the age of 30, and were chosen in a public ceremony held every two months. At this ceremony, eight men were picked by lottery to become the *Priori* (or *Signori*), forming a government called the *Signoria*. Once elected, the *Priori* moved into the Palazzo della Signoria, where they stayed throughout their brief period of office.

Headed by the *Gonfaloniere* (the "Standard-Bearer"), the *Signoria* consulted two elected councils, or *Collegi*, as well as committees introduced to deal with specific crises. Permanent officials included the Chancellor (a post once held by Machiavelli) and the *Podestà*, a magistrate brought in from a neighbouring city as an independent arbitrator. In times of extreme crisis all male citizens over the age of 14 (apart from clerics) were summoned to a *Parlamento* in Piazza della Signoria. When a two-thirds quorum was reached, the people were asked to approve a *Balìa*, a committee to deal with the situation as it saw fit.

All this looked good on paper, but political cliques had few problems ensuring that only likely supporters found their way into the lottery process. If a rogue candidate slipped through the net, or things went awry, then a *Parlamento* was summoned, and the resulting *Balìa* replaced the offending person with a more pliable candidate. It was by such means that the mercantile dynasties – the Peruzzi, the Albizzi, the Strozzi and of course the Medici – retained their power even when not technically in office.

THE SIEGE OF FLORENCE, IN THE PALAZZO VECCHIO

PIAZZA DELLA SIGNORIA AND AROUND

THE PALAZZO VECCHIO

Piazza della Signoria Ⓦ museicivicifiorentini
.it. April–Sept Mon–Wed & Fri–Sun 9am–
midnight (tower closes at 9pm), Thurs closes
2pm; Oct–March Mon–Wed & Fri–Sun
9am–7pm (tower closes at 5pm), Thurs closes
2pm. €6.50. MAP P.42, POCKET MAP C12–D13

Florence's fortress-like **town hall**, the Palazzo Vecchio, was begun in the last year of the thirteenth century, as the home of the *Priori*, or *Signoria*, the highest tier of the city's republican government (see box, p.43). In 1540 Cosimo I moved his retinue here from the Palazzo Medici and grafted a huge extension onto the rear of the building. The Medici remained in residence for only nine years before moving to the Palazzo Pitti – that's when the "old" (*vecchio*) palace acquired its present name.

Work on the beautiful inner **courtyard** was begun by Michelozzo in 1453; the overdone decoration was largely added by Vasari on the occasion of Francesco de' Medici's marriage to Johanna of Austria in 1565.

Vasari was given full rein in the huge **Salone del Cinquecento** at the top of the stairs. The chamber might have had one of Italy's most remarkable decorative schemes: Leonardo da Vinci and Michelangelo were employed to paint frescoes on opposite sides of the room, but Leonardo's work, *The Battle of Anghiari*, was abandoned after his experimental technique went wrong, while Michelangelo's *The Battle of Cascina* had not left the drawing board when he was summoned to Rome by Pope Julius II in 1506. Instead, the hall received six drearily bombastic murals (1563–65) – painted either by Vasari or under his direction – illustrating Florentine military triumphs over Pisa and Siena. It has generally been assumed that Vasari obliterated whatever remained of Leonardo's fresco before beginning his work, but the discovery of a cavity behind *The Battle of Marciano* has raised the possibility that Vasari instead constructed a false wall for his fresco, to preserve his great predecessor's painting. Investigations are proceeding.

The **sculptural highlight** is Michelangelo's *Victory*, almost opposite the entrance door. Carved for the tomb of Pope Julius II, the statue was donated to the Medici by the artist's nephew, then installed here by Vasari in 1565 to celebrate Cosimo's defeat of the Sienese ten years earlier. Directly

THE SALONE DEL CINQUECENTO

Percorsi Segreti

The Palazzo Vecchio's Percorsi Segreti ("Secret Passageways") allow guided-tour access (€6.50) to parts of the building that are normally off limits, such as the beautiful Studiolo di Francesco I and the extraordinary space between the roof and ceiling of the Salone del Cinquecento. The tour lasts an hour and a half and is given at least four times a day; there's usually at least one tour in English every day. Places must be reserved at the Palazzo Vecchio ticket office or by calling ☎ 055 276 8224. There's more info at ⓦ palazzovecchio-family museum.it.

opposite is the plaster model of a companion piece for the *Victory*, Giambologna's *Virtue Overcoming Vice*, another metaphor for Florentine military might.

From the Salone del Cinquecento, a roped-off door allows a glimpse of the most bizarre room in the building, the **Studiolo di Francesco I**. Designed by Vasari and decorated by no fewer than thirty Mannerist artists (1570–74), this windowless cell was created as a retreat for the introverted son of Cosimo and Eleanor, whose portraits face each other across the room.

Upstairs, in the six rooms of the Quartiere di Eleonora di Toledo, the star turn is the tiny and exquisite **Cappella di Eleonora**, vividly decorated in glassy Mannerist style by Bronzino in the 1540s. The **Sala dell'Udienza**, which was originally the audience chamber of the Republic, boasts a stunning gilt-coffered ceiling by Giuliano da Maiano, who was also responsible, with his brother Benedetto, for the intarsia work on the doors and the lovely doorway that leads into the **Sala dei Gigli**, a room that takes its name from the lilies (*gigli*) that adorn most of its surfaces. The room has another splendid ceiling by the Maiano brothers, and a fresco by Domenico Ghirlandaio of *SS Zenobius,*

Stephen and Lorenzo (1481–85), but the undoubted highlight here is Donatello's original *Judith and Holofernes* (1455–60).

Outside the Sala dei Gigli, a staircase leads to the **tower** of Palazzo Vecchio (€6.50, or €10 for the Palazzo Vecchio plus the tower); a 223-step climb takes you to the terrace immediately underneath the bell chambers, passing the prison cell known ironically as the Alberghinetto (Little Hotel), where Cosimo il Vecchio and Savonarola were both held for a while.

The route out of the palazzo takes you past the rooms containing the Loeser collection, which includes a characteristically weird *Passion of Christ* by Piero di Cosimo and Bronzino's portrait of the poet Laura Battiferri.

THE PALAZZO VECCHIO

THE UFFIZI

Piazzale degli Uffizi ⊘ 011uffizi.firenze.it.
Tues–Sun 8.15am–6.50pm; in high summer
and at festive periods it sometimes stays open
until 10pm. €6.50, or €11 when special
exhibitions are on. MAP P.42, POCKET MAP C13

The **Galleria degli Uffizi** is
housed in what were once
government offices (*uffizi*) built
by Vasari for Cosimo I, which
later became the home of the
Medici's art collection. In the
nineteenth century a large
proportion of the statuary was
transferred to the Bargello,
while most of the antiquities
went to the Museo Archeo-
logico, leaving the Uffizi as
essentially a stupendous gallery
of paintings supplemented with
some classical sculptures.

The parade of masterpieces
begins immediately, with
altarpieces of the *Maestà*
(Madonna Enthroned) by
Duccio, **Cimabue** and **Giotto**.
Painters from fourteenth-
century Siena fill **Room 3**,
where you'll see several pieces
by Ambrogio and Pietro
Lorenzetti, and **Simone
Martini**'s glorious *Annunciation*. Soon after comes a display
of paintings that mark the
summit of the precious style
known as International Gothic;
the outstanding pieces here are
Lorenzo Monaco's *Coronation
of the Virgin* (1415) and the

Adoration of the Magi (1423)
by **Gentile da Fabriano**.

The huge diversity of early
Renaissance painting is evident
in Room 7, where **Fra'
Angelico**, **Paolo Uccello** and
Domenico Veneziano are on
display. Veneziano's greatest
pupil, **Piero della Francesca**, is
represented in **Room 8** by the
paired portraits of *Federico da
Montefeltro* and *Battista Sforza*.
Most space in this room is
given over to **Filippo Lippi**,
whose *Madonna and Child with
Two Angels* supplies one of the
gallery's most popular faces:
the model was Lucrezia Buti, a
convent novice with whom he
produced a son, **Filippino
"Little Philip" Lippi**, whose
lustrous *Madonna degli Otto*
hangs nearby.

A staggering array of work by
Filippo Lippi's pupil, **Botticelli**,
fills the largest room in the
Uffizi. *The Primavera* and *The
Birth of Venus* are the
crowd-pullers, but don't
overlook Botticelli's wonderful
religious paintings, such as the
Madonna of the Magnificat and
the *Madonna of the
Pomegranate* – and give some
time to the beautiful *Adoration
of the Shepherds* by his Flemish
contemporary **Hugo van der
Goes**.

Works in Room 15 trace the
formative years of **Leonardo da**

Uffizi practicalities

Queues for on-the-day admission to the Uffizi in high season take
hours to move, so in summer you'd be mad not to pay the €4
surcharge for booking a ticket in advance. Tickets can be reserved
at the Uffizi, or at the Firenze Musei ticket booths at Orsanmichele
(Mon–Sat 9am–4.15pm) and the Libreria My Accademia, Via Ricasoli 105r
(Tues–Sun 8.15am–5.30pm), or by calling ☎ 055 294 883. Even if you have
bought an advance ticket, get there half an hour before your allotted
admission time, because the queues are often enormous. Full admission
costs €6.50 but EU citizens aged 18–25 pay half-price and entry is free to
under-18s and over-65s.

MICHELANGELO ROOM IN THE UFFIZI

Vinci, whose distinctive touch appears first in the *Baptism of Christ* (in Room 14) by his master Verrocchio: the angel in profile and the misty landscape in the background were by the 18-year-old apprentice. A similar terrain of soft-focus mountains and water occupies the far distance in Leonardo's *Annunciation*, which offers a total contrast to his sketch of the *Adoration of the Magi,* where the infant Christ occupies the eye of a vortex of figures.

Most of the rest of the room is given over to Raphael's teacher, **Perugino**, whose brilliance as a portraitist is demonstrated later. **Room 18**, the octagonal **Tribuna**, houses the most important of the Medici's collection of **classical sculptures**, chief among which is the *Medici Venus*.

Wonderful pieces by **Cranach** and **Dürer** are still to come, along with exquisite small paintings by **Mantegna** and **Michelangelo**'s *Doni Tondo*, the only easel painting he ever came close to finishing. Another of the colossal figures of the sixteenth century, **Titian**, appears in a room that has no fewer than eleven of his paintings, and beyond the

section devoted to Emilian painters such as **Parmigianino** you come to more artists from Venice and the Veneto, with outstanding works by **Moroni, Paolo Veronese, Lotto** and **Tintoretto**.

When the huge suite of new galleries on the lower floor is completed, much of the work by Italian artists of the sixteenth and seventeenth centuries will be moved downstairs, along with most of the non-Italian paintings. Magnificent canvases by **Andrea del Sarto, Rosso Fiorentino, Pontormo, Bronzino** and **Caravaggio** have already been relocated, and Raphael has a room all to himself, featuring a self-portrait, the lovely *Madonna of the Goldfinch* and *Pope Leo X with Cardinals Giulio de' Medici and Luigi de' Rossi* – as shifty a group of ecclesiastics as was ever gathered in one frame. The Uffizi's huge collection of pictures from the Netherlands includes work by Rubens, Van Dyck and Rembrandt, while Goya, El Greco and Velasquez are in the Spanish rooms. In the French section, Watteau and Chardin provide some of the highlights.

The Corridoio Vasariano

The Corridoio Vasariano, a **passageway** built by Vasari in 1565 to link the Palazzo Vecchio to the Palazzo Pitti through the Uffizi, is lined with paintings, the larger portion of which comprises a gallery of self-portraits that's littered with illustrious names: Andrea del Sarto, Bronzino, Bernini, Rubens, Rembrandt, Velázquez, David, Delacroix and Ingres. It's intended that these paintings will eventually be rehung on the first floor of the expanded Uffizi.

Because of staff shortages and strict limits on numbers allowed into the corridor (there is no fire escape), access is difficult. At the time of writing, tours are offered to groups of 10 people or more, at a charge of €240 per group – and every member also has to pay for admission to the Uffizi, as the tour begins inside the gallery. Various private agencies can also arrange tours, but they charge exorbitant rates of around €90 per person.

THE MUSEO GALILEO

Piazza dei Giudici 1 ⓦ museogalileo.it. Mon & Wed–Sun 9.30am–6pm, Tues 9.30am–1pm. €9. MAP P.42, POCKET MAP C13

Long after Florence had declined from its artistic apogee, the intellectual reputation of the city was maintained by its scientists, many of them directly encouraged by the ruling Medici-Lorraine dynasty. Two of the latter, Grand Duke Ferdinando II and his brother Leopoldo, both of whom studied with Galileo, founded a scientific academy at the Pitti in 1657. Called the Accademia del Cimento (Academy of Experiment), its motto was "Try and try again." The instruments made and acquired by this academy are the core of the city's **science museum**, recently rebranded as the Museo Galileo.

Some of Galileo's original instruments are on show on the first floor, such as the lens with which he discovered the four moons of Jupiter, which he tactfully named the Medicean planets. (An enormous lodestone given by Galileo to Ferdinando II is on display by the ticket desk.) On this floor you'll also find the museum's **holy relics** – bones from two of Galileo's fingers, plus a tooth. Other cases are filled with beautiful Arab astrolabes, calculating machines, early telescopes, and some delicate and ornate thermometers. The most imposing single exhibit on this floor is a massive **armillary sphere** made in 1593 for Ferdinando I to provide a visual proof of the supposed veracity of the earth-centred Ptolemaic system.

ARMILLARY SPHERE IN THE MUSEO GALILEO

On the floor above there are all kinds of exquisitely manufactured scientific and mechanical equipment, several built to demonstrate the fundamental laws of physics. Dozens of clocks and timepieces are on show too, along with some spectacular electrical machines, and a huge lens made for Cosimo III, with which Faraday and Davy managed to ignite a diamond by focusing the rays of the sun. At the end there's a medical section full of alarming surgical instruments and anatomical wax models for teaching obstetrics, plus the contents of a medieval pharmacy, displaying such unlikely cure-alls as *Sangue del Drago* (Dragon's Blood) and *Confetti di Seme Santo* (Confections of Blessed Semen).

THE BADÌA FIORENTINA

Via del Proconsolo. Open to tourists Mon 3–6pm. Free. MAP P.42, POCKET MAP D12

The Badìa Fiorentina is one of the most impressive churches in the centre of the city, and is a place of special significance for admirers of Dante: the poet worshipped here, and this was also where Boccaccio delivered his celebrated lectures on Dante's epic.

Founded in 978 by Willa, widow of the Margrave of Tuscany, in honour of her husband, the Badìa was one of the focal buildings in medieval Florence: the city's sick were treated in a **hospital** founded here in 1031, while the main bell marked the divisions of the working day. The hospital owed much to Willa's son, Ugo, who further endowed his mother's foundation after a vision of the hellish torments that awaited him by "reason of his worldly

THE BADÌA FIORENTINA

life, unless he should repent". Inside the church you'll find the tomb monument to Ugo, sculpted by Mino da Fiesole between 1469 and 1481. The other outstanding work of art is Filippino Lippi's superb *Apparition of the Virgin to St Bernard* (c. 1485), in which Bernard is shown in the act of writing a homily aimed at those caught between the "rocks" of tribulation and the "chains" of sin; the presence of the four monks reinforces the message that redemption lies in the contemplative life.

A staircase leads from the choir to the upper storey of the **Chiostro degli Aranci** (Cloister of the Oranges), named after the fruit trees that used to be grown here. Two of its flanks are graced with an anonymous but highly distinctive fresco cycle (1436–39) on the life of St Benedict. A later panel, showing the saint throwing himself into bushes to resist temptation, is by the young Bronzino.

THE BARGELLO

Via del Proconsolo 4 ⓦ uffizi.firenze.it.
Tues–Sat 8.15am–2pm, plus second & fourth
Sun of month and first, and third & fifth Mon
of month, same hours, with longer hours (and
higher admission charge) for special
exhibitions. €4. MAP P.42, POCKET MAP D12

The Museo Nazionale del Bargello occupies the dour Palazzo del Bargello, which was built in 1255 and soon became the seat of the *Podestà*, the city's chief magistrate, and the site of the main law court. The building acquired its present name after 1574, when the Medici abolished the post of *Podestà* and the building became home to the chief of police – the *Bargello*.

You've no time to catch your breath in the Bargello: the room immediately behind the ticket office is crammed with treasures, chief of which are the work of **Michelangelo**, in whose shadow every Florentine sculptor laboured.

The tipsy, soft-bellied figure of *Bacchus* (1496–97) was his first major sculpture, carved at the age of 22, a year or so before his great *Pietà* in Rome. Michelangelo's style soon evolved into something less ostentatiously virtuosic, as is shown by the tender *Tondo*

Pitti (1503–05), while the rugged expressivity of his late manner is exemplified by the square-jawed *Bust of Brutus* (c.1540), the artist's sole work of this kind. A powerful portrait sketch in stone, it's a coded celebration of anti-Medicean republicanism, carved soon after the murder of the nightmarish Duke Alessandro de' Medici.

Works by Michelangelo's followers and contemporaries are ranged in the immediate vicinity. **Benvenuto Cellini** and **Giambologna** are the best of them, and there's more Giambologna at the top of the courtyard staircase, where the first-floor loggia has been turned into a menagerie for the bronze animals and birds he made for the Medici villa at Castello, just outside Florence.

The doorway to the right opens into the Salone del Consiglio Generale, the museum's second key room, where the presiding genius is **Donatello**, the fountainhead of Renaissance sculpture. In addition to his great statue of *St George* the room holds two figures of *David* – the later one (1430–40) was the first freestanding nude figure created since classical times.

A decade later the sculptor produced the strange prancing figure known as *Amor-Atys*, which was mistaken for a genuine statue from classical antiquity – the highest compliment the artist could have wished for. Donatello was just as comfortable with portraiture as with Christian or pagan imagery, as his breathtakingly vivid terracotta *Bust of Niccolò da Uzzano* demonstrates; it may be the earliest Renaissance portrait bust. When the occasion demanded, Donatello could also produce a straightfor-wardly monumental piece like the nearby *Marzocco* (1418–20), Florence's heraldic lion.

Donatello's master, **Ghiberti**, is represented by his relief of *Abraham's Sacrifice*, his entry in the competition to design the Baptistery doors in 1401 (see p.34), easily missed on the right-hand wall; the treatment of the theme submitted by Brunelleschi, effectively the runner-up, is hung alongside. Set around the walls of the room, a sequence of glazed terracotta Madonnas embodies **Luca della Robbia**'s sweet-natured humanism.

The rest of this floor is occupied by a superb collection of European and Islamic applied art, with dazzling speci-mens of work in enamel, glass, silver, majolica and ivory: among the ivory pieces from Byzantium and medieval France you'll find combs, boxes, chess pieces, and devotional panels featuring scores of figures crammed into a space the size of a paperback.

Sculpture resumes upstairs, with a room largely devoted to the della Robbia family, a prelude to the **Sala dei Bronzetti**, Italy's best assembly

MERCURY BY GIAMBOLOGNA

of small Renaissance bronzes. Also on this floor there's another roomful of della Robbias and a splendid display of bronze medals, featuring specimens from the great pioneer of this form of portable art, Pisanello. Lastly, there's a room devoted mainly to **Renaissance portrait busts**, where the centrepiece is Verrocchio's *David*, clearly influenced by the Donatello figure downstairs. Around the walls you'll find Mino da Fiesole's busts of Giovanni de' Medici and Piero il Gottoso (the sons of Cosimo de' Medici), Antonio del Pollaiuolo's *Young Cavalier* (which is probably another Medici portrait), and a bust labelled *Ritratto d'Ignoto* (Portrait of an Unknown Man), which may in fact depict Macchiavelli. Other outstanding pieces include Francesco Laurana's *Battista Sforza*, the *Woman Holding Flowers* by Verrocchio, and the fraught marble relief in which Verrocchio portrays the death of Francesca Tornabuoni-Pitti, from whose tomb this panel was taken.

Dante

Dante Alighieri was born in 1265 into a minor noble family. He was educated at Bologna and later at Padua, where he studied philosophy and astronomy. The defining moment in his life came in 1274 when he met the 8-year-old **Beatrice Portinari**. Himself aged just 9 at the time, Dante later described the encounter by quoting the words of Homer: "She appeared to be born not of mortal man but of God." Unhappily, Beatrice's family had decided their daughter was to marry someone else – Simone de' Bardi. The ceremony took place when she was 17; seven years later she was dead. Dante, for his part, had been promised – aged 12 – to Gemma Donati. The wedding took place in 1295, when the poet was 30.

His romantic hopes dashed, Dante settled down to a military and political career. In 1289 he fought for Florence against Arezzo and helped in a campaign against Pisa. Eleven years later he was dispatched to San Gimignano, where he was entrusted with the job of coaxing the town into an alliance against Pope Boniface VIII, who had designs on Tuscany. In June of the same year he sought to settle the widening breach between the Black (anti-imperial) and White (more conciliatory) factions of Florence's ruling Guelph party. The Black Guelphs eventually emerged triumphant, and Dante's White sympathies sealed his fate. In 1302, following trumped-up charges of corruption, he was sentenced with other Whites to two years' exile. Rejecting his city of "self-made men and fast-got gain", Dante wandered between Forlì, Verona, Padua, Luni and Venice, writing much of **The Divine Comedy** as he went, before finally settling in Ravenna, where he died in 1321.

Running to more than 14,000 lines, *La Commedia* (the *Divina* was added after Dante's death) is an extraordinarily rich allegory, recounting the poet's journey through *Inferno* (Hell), *Purgatorio* (Purgatory), and *Paradiso* (Paradise), accompanied initially by the Roman poet Virgil and then by Beatrice. Each of these three realms of the dead is depicted in 33 *canti* (a "prologue" to the *Inferno* brings the total up to 100), composed in a verse scheme called *terza rima*, in which lines of eleven syllables follow the rhyme scheme aba, bcb, cdc, ded, etc. Within this framework Dante achieves an amazing variety of tone, encompassing everything from the desperate abuse of the damned to the exalted lyricism of his vision of heaven. Equally remarkable is the fact that Dante wrote his poem in the Tuscan dialect, at a time when Latin was regarded as the only language suitable for serious subjects. Before *La Commedia*, Tuscan was the language of the street; afterwards, it began to be seen as the language of all Italian people, from peasants to philosophers.

THE CASA DI DANTE

Via Santa Margherita 1 ⓦ museocasadidante
.it. Tues–Sun 10am–5pm. €4. MAP P.42,
POCKET MAP D11

Fraudulently marketed as
Dante's house, the Casa di
Dante is actually a medieval
pastiche dating from 1910. The
museum is a homage to the
poet rather than a shrine: it
contains nothing directly
related to his life, and it's likely
Dante was born not on this site
but somewhere in the street
that bears his name. Many
editions of the *Divina
Commedia* are on show, with
copies of Botticelli's illustra-
tions to the poem and a variety
of context-setting displays.

SANTA MARGHERITA DE' CERCHI

Via Santa Margherita. Mon–Thurs & Sat
10am–noon & 3–5pm, Fri 10am–noon. Free.
MAP P.42, POCKET MAP D11

Folklore has it that Dante
married his wife, Gemma
Donati, in the eleventh-century
church of Santa Margherita de'
Cerchi. There's no evidence for
the claim, but the building does
contain tombs belonging to the
Portinari, Beatrice's family; the
porch also features the Donati
family crest, as this was their

local parish church. The church
is worth a look chiefly for its
altarpiece of the *Madonna and
Four Saints* by Neri di Bicci.

SAN MARTINO DEL VESCOVO

Piazza San Martino. Mon–Thurs 10am–noon
& 3–5pm, Fri 10am–noon. Free. MAP P.42,
POCKET MAP C12–D12

The tiny San Martino del
Vescovo stands on the site of an
oratory that served as the
Alighieris' parish church.
Rebuilt in 1479, it later became
the headquarters of the
Compagnia di Buonomini, a
charitable body dedicated to
aiding impoverished citizens
for whom begging was too
demeaning. The Buonomini
commissioned from Ghirlandaio's workshop a sequence of
frescoes showing altruistic acts
and scenes from the life of St
Martin, and the result is an
absorbing record of daily life in
Renaissance Florence.

THE TORRE DELLA CASTAGNA

Piazza San Martino. MAP P.42, POCKET MAP D11–D12

Opposite San Martino del
Vescovo soars the thirteenth-
century Torre della Castagna,
meeting place of the city's
Priori before they decamped to
the Palazzo Vecchio. This is one
of the most striking remnants
of Florence's medieval
townscape, when more than
150 such towers rose between
the river and the Duomo, many
of them over two hundred feet
high. Allied clans would link
their towers with **wooden
catwalks**, creating a sort of
upper-class promenade above
the heads of the lowlier
citizens. In 1250 the government of the *Primo Popolo*
ordered that the towers be
reduced by two-thirds of their
height; the resulting rubble was
voluminous enough to extend
the city walls beyond the Arno.

SAN MARTINO DEL VESCOVO

ORSANMICHELE

Via dei Calzaiuoli. Daily 10am–5pm. Free.
MAP P.42, POCKET MAP C12

Looming like a fortress over Via dei Calzaiuoli, the foursquare **Orsanmichele** is the oddest church in Florence – a unique hybrid of the sacred and secular, it resembles no other church in the city, and it's not even immediately apparent which of its walls is the front. It's a major monument in itself, and its exterior was once the most impressive outdoor sculpture gallery in the city. Nowadays all of the pieces outside are replicas; most of the originals are in the attached museum.

The first building here was a small oratory secreted in the vegetable garden (*orto*) of a now-vanished Benedictine monastery. A larger church stood on the site from the ninth century: San Michele ad Hortum, later San Michele in Orte – hence the compacted form of Orsanmichele. This church was replaced by a grain market in the thirteenth century, and this in turn was replaced by a loggia designed to serve as a trade hall for the *Arti Maggiori*, the Great Guilds which governed the city. Between 1367 and 1380 the loggia was walled in, after which the site was again dedicated almost exclusively to religious functions, while the two upper storeys were used as emergency grain stores. It was the guilds who paid for the sculptures, which include Ghiberti's *John the Baptist* (the earliest life-size bronze statue of the Renaissance), Verrocchio's *The Incredulity of St Thomas*, Brunelleschi's *St Peter*, and Donatello's *St George* and *St Mark*.

Inside, the centrepiece is a pavilion-sized glass and marble **tabernacle** by Orcagna, the only significant sculptural work by the artist. Decorated with lapis lazuli, stained glass and gold, it frames a Madonna painted in 1347 by Bernardo Daddi as a replacement for the miraculous image of the Virgin, which was destroyed by a fire in 1304. The brotherhood that administered Orsanmichele paid for the tabernacle from thanksgiving donations in the aftermath of the Black Death; so many people attributed their survival to the Madonna's intervention that the money received in 1348 alone was greater than the annual tax income of the city coffers.

Upstairs, the vaulted halls of the granary house the **Museo di Orsanmichele** (Mon 10am–5pm; free), which is entered via the footbridge from the Palazzo dell'Arte della Lana, the building opposite the church entrance. The hall itself is remarkable, and it's home to the original versions of most of the most important exterior statues.

ORSANMICHELE

Shops

COIN

Via dei Calzaiuoli 56r ☎ 055 280 531, 🖤 coin
.it. Mon–Sat 10am–8pm, Sun 11am–8pm.
MAP P.42, POCKET MAP C11

A clothes-dominated chain
store in an excellent central
position. Quality is generally
high, though styles are fairly
conservative except for one or
two youth-oriented franchises
on the ground floor. Also a
good place for linen and other
household goods.

SPEZIERIA ERBORISTA PALAZZO VECCHIO

Via Vacchereccia 9r ☎ 055 239 6055. July &
Aug Mon–Fri 9am–7.30pm, Sat 9am–5pm;
Sept–June Mon–Sat 9.30am–7.30pm, plus
first and last Sun of month 1.30–7pm.
MAP P.42, POCKET MAP C12

A celebrated old shop selling
its own range of unique
perfumes, such as Acqua di
Caterina de' Medici.

Gelateria

PERCHÈ NO!

Via de' Tavolini 19r. March–Oct Mon &
Wed–Sat 11am–midnight, Tues noon–8pm;
Dec–Feb Mon & Wed–Sat noon–7.30pm;
closed Nov. MAP P.42, POCKET MAP C11

A superb *gelateria*, in business
since the 1930s; go for the
crema, the chocolate or the
gorgeous pistachio.

Cafés, bars & snacks

ALL'ANTICO TRIPPAIO

Piazza dei Cimatori. Mon–Fri 8.30am–8.30pm;
closed last week of July and first 3 weeks of
Aug. MAP P.42, POCKET MAP C11

This stall specializes in a local
delicacy called *lampredotto*: hot
tripe served in a bun with a
spicy sauce. Tripe salads are
available in summer, while the
less adventurous can go for
cold cuts of *porchetta*
(spit-roast pork).

ALL'ANTICO VINAIO

Via dei Neri 65r. Mon–Sat 8am–10pm; closed
3 weeks in late July & early Aug. MAP P.42,
POCKET MAP D13

Though recently revamped,
this place – located between
the Uffizi and Santa Croce
– preserves much of the
rough-and-ready atmosphere
that's made it one of Florence's
most popular wine bars for
the last hundred years. Also
serves coffee, rolls and plates
of pasta.

CANTINETTA DEI VERRAZZANO

Via de' Tavolini 18–20r ☎ 055 268 590. July
& Aug Mon–Sat 8am–4pm; Sept–June
Mon–Sat 8am–9pm. MAP P.42, POCKET MAP C11

Owned by Castello dei
Verrazzano, a major Chianti
vineyard, this wood-panelled
place near Orsanmichele is
part-bar, part-café and
part-bakery, making its own
excellent pizza, *focaccia* and
cakes. A perfect spot for a light
lunch or an early evening glass.

ICE CREAM FROM PERCHÈ NO!

I FRATELLINI

Via dei Cimatori 38r. Daily 9am–8pm.
MAP P.42, POCKET MAP C12

This minuscule stand-up bar – which attracts a melée most lunchtimes – has been in operation since the 1870s; Armando and Michele, the current proprietors, serve 29 varieties of panini, and local wines by the glass.

'INO

Via de' Georgofili 3–7r ☎ 055 219 208, Ⓦ inofirenze.com. Daily 11.30am–4.30pm. MAP P.42, POCKET MAP C13

Part-delicatessen, part-sandwich bar, 'Ino serves what are possibly the most delectable panini in Florence, all made to order, using only the finest ingredients; the wine on offer is similarly fine.

RIVOIRE

Piazza della Signoria 5r ☎ 055 221 4412, Ⓦ rivoire.it. Tues–Sun 8am–midnight. MAP P.42, POCKET MAP C12

If you want to people-watch on Florence's main square, this is the place to do so, and the outside tables are invariably packed. Founded in 1872, the café started life specializing in hot chocolate, and chocolate is still its main claim to fame. Ice creams are also good, but the sandwiches and snacks are grotesquely overpriced.

Restaurants

ANTICO FATTORE

Via Lambertesca 1–3r ☎ 055 288 975, Ⓦ anticofattore.it. Mon–Sat noon–2.45pm & 7–10.30pm; closed Aug. MAP P.42, POCKET MAP C13

Simple Tuscan dishes dominate the menu at this classic Florentine trattoria, which has barely changed its look since the 1920s. With main courses well under €20, it's remarkable value for this central locality.

GUSTAVINO

Via della Condotta 37r ☎ 055 239 9806, Ⓦ gustavino.it. Daily 7–11.30pm, plus Sat & Sun noon–3.30pm. MAP P.42, POCKET MAP C12

With its steel chairs and glass-topped tables, this *enoteca con cucina* might be a bit too clinical for some tastes, but it has a fine selection of wines, and the kitchen (which is on full view, both from the tables and from the street) turns out some very interesting dishes. Main courses are in the region of €20–25. Less-pricy snacks and light meals are offered at its

RIVOIRE

excellent wine shop next door, called *Canova*.

ORA D'ARIA

Via dei Georgofili 11r ☎ 055 200 1699. Ⓦ www.oradariaristorante.com. Mon 7.30–10pm, Tues–Sat 12.30–2.30pm & 7.30–10pm; closed two weeks Aug. MAP P.42, POCKET MAP C13

Marco Stabile, the young boss of *Ora d'Aria*, has rapidly established a reputation as one of the city's best restaurateurs, thanks to menus that offer a high-quality mix of the traditional and the innovative. The tasting menus (€50–75) are very good value for such exceptional cooking; à la carte, main courses are in excess of €30 – if you go for the *bistecca alla fiorentina* you'll be paying in the region of €50 each. The bright and cool setting is the very opposite of the faux-rustic style you often find elsewhere in Florence.

VINI E VECCHI SAPORI

Via dei Magazzini 3r ☎ 055 293 045. Tues–Sat 12.30–2.30pm & 7.30–10pm, Sun 12.30–2.30pm only. MAP P.42, POCKET MAP D12

Located just a few yards off the piazza, this tiny family-run trattoria is always packed – which is hardly surprising, as it offers four-square traditional Florentine food at prices much lower than its more high-toned neighbours.

YELLOW BAR

Via del Proconsolo 39r ☎ 055 211 766. Mon & Wed–Sun noon–3pm & 7pm–midnight, Tues noon–3pm. MAP P.42, POCKET MAP D11

This place looks like a fast-food joint, but the queues of Florentines waiting for a table give you a clue that first impressions are misleading. Inside, the convivial atmosphere in the large dining room is matched by superlative pan-Italian food (including

YELLOW BAR

excellent pizzas) in large portions at very reasonable prices. When the main dining room is busy you can often get a table in the mildly less appealing rooms downstairs.

Clubs

BLOB CLUB

Via Vinegia 21r ☎ 055 211 209. Oct–April daily 6pm–4am. MAP P.42, POCKET MAP D13

A favourite with Florentine students, possibly on account of its free admission and the 6–9pm happy hour. Seating upstairs, bar and tiny dancefloor downstairs, but don't expect to do much dancing – later on, especially on weekend nights, *Blob* gets packed full with a very happy and very drunken crowd.

TABASCO

Piazza Santa Cecilia 3r ☎ 055 213 000, Ⓦ tabascogay.it. Tues–Sun 10pm–6am; music Thurs–Sun. MAP P.42, POCKET MAP C12

One of the first gay clubs in Italy, now in operation for more than thirty years. The small dancefloor gets particularly packed on weekend nights.

West of the centre

Despite the urban improvement schemes of the nineteenth century and the damage inflicted during World War II, several of the streets immediately to the west of Piazza della Signoria retain their medieval character: an amble along Via Porta Rossa, Via delle Terme and Borgo Santi Apostoli will give you some idea of the feel of Florence in the Middle Ages, when every big house was an urban fortress. The best-preserved of these medieval redoubts is the Palazzo Davanzati, whose interior looks little different from the way it did six hundred years ago. The exquisite ancient church of Santi Apostoli is nearby, as is the church of Santa Trinita, which is home to an outstanding fresco cycle by Domenico Ghirlandaio. Beyond the glitzy Via de' Tornabuoni – the city's priciest slice of retail real estate – you'll find Ognissanti, which also has some outstanding paintings, but the major monument in this area is the fresco-filled church of Santa Maria Novella, which stands opposite the train station.

THE MERCATO NUOVO

Piazza di Mercato Nuovo. Mid-Feb to mid-Nov daily 9am–7pm; mid-Nov to mid-Feb Tues–Sat 9am–5pm. MAP P.60–61. POCKET MAP B12

The Mercato Nuovo, or Mercato del Porcellino, has been the site of a market since the eleventh century, though the present loggia dates from the sixteenth. Having forked out their euros at the souvenir stalls, most people join the small group that's invariably gathered round the bronze boar known as *Il Porcellino*: you're supposed to earn good luck by

IL PORCELLINO

getting a coin to fall from the animal's mouth through the grille below his head.

PALAZZO DAVANZATI

Via Porta Rossa 13 ⓦ uffizi.firenze.it. Tues & Thurs–Sat 8.15am–1.50pm, Wed 8.15am–7pm, plus second & fourth Mon of month & first, third and fifth Sun 8.15am–1.50pm. €2. Visitors have unrestricted access to the first floor; visits to the second and third floors are at 10am, 11am & noon, and must be pre-booked in person or by phone. MAP P.60–61, POCKET MAP B12

Virtually every room of the fourteenth-century Palazzo Davanzati is furnished and decorated in medieval style, using genuine artefacts gathered from a variety of sources.

Merchants' houses in that period would typically have had elaborately **painted walls** in the main rooms, and the Palazzo Davanzati preserves some fine examples of such decor – especially in the dining room. Before the development of systems of credit, wealth had to be sunk into assets such as the tapestries, ceramics, sculpture and lacework that alleviate the austerity of many of these rooms; any surplus cash would have been locked away in a strongbox like the extraordinary example in the **Sala Piccola**. There's also a fine collection of *cassoni*, the painted chests in which the wife's dowry would be stored.

Plushest of the rooms is the first-floor bedroom, but the spot where the occupants would have been likeliest to linger is the **kitchen**. Located on the top floor to minimize the damage that might be caused by the outbreak of a fire, it would have been the warmest room in the house. A load of ancient utensils are on show here, and set into one wall there is the most civilized of amenities, a service

SANTI APOSTOLI

shaft connecting the kitchen to all floors of the building. The leaded glass would have been considered a marvel at a time when many windows were covered with turpentine-soaked rags stretched across frames to repel rainwater.

SANTI APOSTOLI

Piazza del Limbo. Mon–Sat 10am–noon & 4–5.30pm, Sun 4–5.30pm. Free. MAP P.60–61, POCKET MAP B12–B13

Legend has it that the church of Santi Apostoli was founded by Charlemagne; it's not quite that ancient, but certainly pre-dates the end of the first millennium. Side chapels were added in the fifteenth and sixteenth centuries, yet the building still has an austere beauty quite unlike any other church in the city centre, with its expanses of bare stone wall and columns of green Prato marble.

The chief treasures of Santi Apostoli are some stone fragments from the Holy Sepulchre in Jerusalem, which on Holy Saturday are used to spark the flame that ignites the "dove" which in turn sets off the fireworks in front of the Duomo.

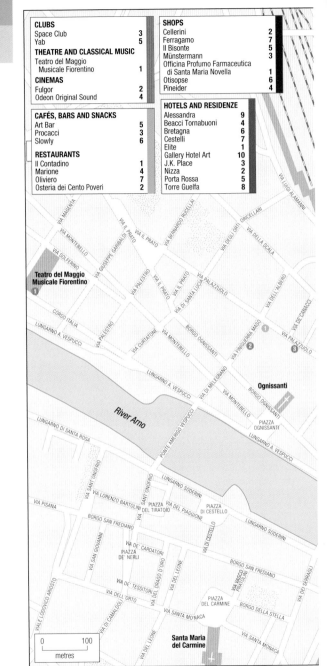

CLUBS

Space Club	3
Yab	5

THEATRE AND CLASSICAL MUSIC

Teatro del Maggio Musicale Fiorentino	1

CINEMAS

Fulgor	2
Odeon Original Sound	4

CAFÉS, BARS AND SNACKS

Art Bar	5
Procacci	3
Slowly	6

RESTAURANTS

Il Contadino	1
Marione	4
Oliviero	7
Osteria dei Cento Poveri	2

SHOPS

Cellerini	2
Ferragamo	7
Il Bisonte	5
Münstermann	3
Officina Profumo Farmaceutica di Santa Maria Novella	1
Otisope	6
Pineider	4

HOTELS AND RESIDENZE

Alessandra	9
Beacci Tornabuoni	4
Bretagna	6
Cestelli	7
Elite	1
Gallery Hotel Art	10
J.K. Place	3
Nizza	2
Porta Rossa	5
Torre Guelfa	8

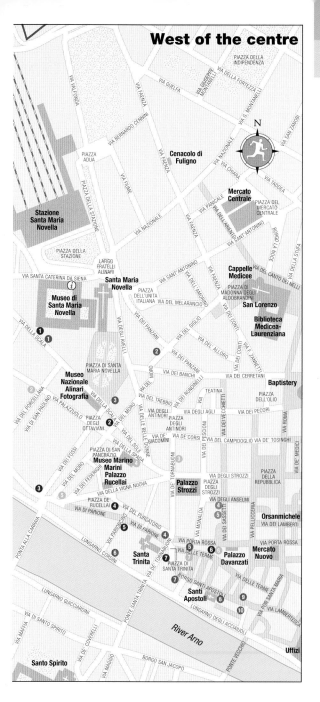

West of the centre

PIAZZA DELLA
INDIPENDENZA

VIA GIUSEPPE MONTANELLI

VIA DELLA FORTEZZA

VIA G. MONTANELLI

VIA VALFONDA

VIA GUELFA

VIA BERNARDO CENNINI

VIA FAENZA

VIA SAN ZANOBI

PIAZZA
ADUA

Cenacolo di Fuligno

VIA FAENZA

VIA NAZIONALE

VIA CHIARA

VIA TADDEA

VIA FIUME

PIAZZA DELLA STAZIONE

Mercato Centrale

PIAZZA DEL MERCATO CENTRALE

BORGO LA NOCE

VIA DELLA STUFA

Stazione Santa Maria Novella

VIA NAZIONALE

VIA FAENZA

VIA PANICALE

VIA DELL'ARIENTO

VIA SANT'ANTONINO

VIA DEL CANTO DEI NELLI

PIAZZA DELLA STAZIONE

LARGO FRATELLI ALINARI

VIA SANTA CATERINA DA SIENA

(i)

Santa Maria Novella

PIAZZA DELL'UNITA ITALIANA

VIA SANT'ANTONINO

VIA DELL'AMORINO

VIA FAENZA

Cappelle Medicee

PIAZZA DI MADONNA DEGLI ALDOBRANDINI

VIA DEL MELARANCIO

San Lorenzo

VIA DEI CONTI

VIA F. ZANNETTI

Museo di Santa Maria Novella

VIA DELLA SCALA

VIA DEGLI AVELLI

VIA DEL GIGLIO

Biblioteca Medicea-Laurenziana

① ①

VIA DEI PANZANI

VIA DEL'ALLORO

PIAZZA DI SANTA MARIA NOVELLA

②

VIA DEI PANZANI

VIA DEI CONTI

VIA DELLA SCALA

VIA DEL MORO

VIA DEI BANCHI

VIA DEI CERRETANI

Baptistery

② ②

Museo Nazionale Alinari Fotografia

③

VIA DELLA SCALA

VIA DEL TREBBIO

VIA DEI RONDINELLI

TEATINA

PIAZZA DELL'OLIO

VIA DELLA PORCELLANA

VIA DI SAN PAOLINO

VIA PALAZZUOLO

PIAZZA DEGLI OTTAVIANI

② ②

VIA DEGLI ANTINORI

VIA DEGLI AGLI

VIA DEI VECCHIETTI

VIA DEI PECORI

VIA ROMA

VIA DEL FOSSI

VIA DELLE BELLE DONNE

VIA DEGLI ANTINORI

VIA DE' PESCIONI

VIA DEL CAMPIDOGLIO

VIA DE' TOSINGHI

VIA DE' MEDICI

VIA DE' GIACOMINI

VIA DEI CORSI

VIA DELLA SPADA

PIAZZA DI SAN PANCRAZIO

Museo Marino Marini Palazzo Rucellai

VIA DEI FEDERIGHI

VIA DEL MORO

VIA DELLA VIGNA NUOVA

③

⑤

PIAZZA DE' RUCELLAI

④

VIA DEL PURGATORIO

VIA DEGLI STROZZI

PIAZZA DEGLI STROZZI

PIAZZA DELLA REPUBBLICA

③

Palazzo Strozzi

VIA DE' TORNABUONI

VIA DEGLI ANSELMI

VIA DEI SASSETTI

Orsanmichele

VIA DEI LAMBERTI

③

VIA DI PARIONE

VIA DI PARIONE

VIA DEL PARIONCINO

⑤

④

VIA MONALDA

VIA PELLICCERIA

④

⑤

⑥

VIA PORTA ROSSA

VIA PORTA ROSSA

PONTE ALLA CARRAIA

LUNGARNO CORSINI

⑥

Santa Trinita

VIA DEL PARIONE

④

VIA DELLE TERME

⑥

Palazzo Davanzati

Mercato Nuovo

VIA DELLE TERME

VIA POR SANTA MARIA

PIAZZA DI SANTA TRINITA

⑦

BORGO SANTI APOSTOLI

Santi Apostoli

⑧

⑨

VIA LAMBERTESCA

PONTE SANTA TRINITA

VIA DE' TORNABUONI

LUNGARNO GUICCIARDINI

LUNGARNO DEGLI ACCIAIUOLI

⑩

VIA DI SANTO SPIRITO

VIA MAFFIA

VIA DI COVERELLI

River Arno

Uffizi

PONTE VECCHIO

Santo Spirito

VIA MAGGIO

BORGO SAN JACOPO

SANTA TRÌNITA

Mon–Sat 8am–noon & 4–6pm, Sun 8–10.45am & 4–6pm. Free. MAP P.60–61, POCKET MAP A12

Santa Trìnita was founded in 1092 by a Florentine nobleman called **Giovanni Gualberto**, scenes from whose life are illustrated in the frescoes in the fourth chapel of the left aisle. One Good Friday, so the story goes, Gualberto set off intent on avenging the murder of his brother. On finding the murderer he decided to spare his life – it was Good Friday – and proceeded to San Miniato (see p.116), where a crucifix is said to have bowed its head to honour his act of mercy. Giovanni went on to become a Benedictine monk and founded the reforming Vallombrosan order and – notwithstanding the mayhem created on Florence's streets by his militant supporters – was eventually canonized.

The church was rebuilt between about 1300 and 1330, and piecemeal additions over the years have lent it a pleasantly hybrid air: the largely Gothic interior contrasts with the Mannerist façade, itself at odds with the Romanesque front wall of the interior. The fame of the building is due chiefly to Ghirlandaio's **frescoes** (1483–86) of scenes from the life of St Francis, in the Cappella Sassetti.

Commissioned by Francesco Sassetti, a friend of Lorenzo the Magnificent, these scenes were intended, in part, to eclipse the chapel in Santa Maria Novella sponsored by Sassetti's rival, Giovanni Tornabuoni, which was also painted by Ghirlandaio. St Francis, floating in the sky, is shown bringing a child back to life in Piazza Santa Trìnita, with the church in the background. (Opposite the church you can see the child plummeting to his temporary death.) Above this scene, *St Francis Receiving the Rule* sets the action in Piazza della Signoria and features (right foreground) a portrait of Sassetti between his son, Federigo, and Lorenzo il Magnifico (Sassetti was general manager of the Medici bank). On the steps below them are the humanist Poliziano and three of his pupils, Lorenzo's sons; the blond boy at the back of the line is Giovanni, the future Pope Leo X. Ghirlandaio has depicted himself in the

lower scene, with his hand on his hip, and is also present in the chapel's altarpiece, the *Adoration of the Shepherds* (1485) – he's the shepherd pointing to the Child and, by way of self-identification, to the garland (*ghirlanda*). The figures of the donors – Sassetti and his wife, Nera Corsi – kneel to either side; they are buried in Giuliano da Sangallo's black tombs under the side arches.

Displayed in the neighbouring Cappella Doni is the miraculous crucifix that bowed its head to Gualberto. The third of the church's major works, a powerful composition by Luca della Robbia – the tomb of Benozzo Federighi, bishop of Fiesole – occupies the left wall of the Cappella Scali, the farthest chapel.

PONTE SANTA TRÌNITA

MAP P.60–61, POCKET MAP A12–A13

The sleek Ponte Santa Trìnita was built on Cosimo I's orders after its predecessor was demolished in a flood. The roads on both banks were raised and widened to accentuate the dramatic potential of the new link between the city centre and the Oltrarno, but what makes this the classiest bridge in Florence is the sensuous **curve** of its arches, a curve so shallow that engineers have been baffled as to how the bridge bears up under the strain. Ostensibly the design was devised by **Ammannati**, one of the Medici's favourite artists, but the curves so closely resemble the arc of Michelangelo's Medici tombs that it's likely the credit belongs to him.

In 1944 the Nazis blew the bridge to smithereens and seven years later it was decided to rebuild it using as much of

FERRAGAMO, VIA DE' TORNABUONI

the original material as could be dredged from the Arno. To ensure maximum authenticity, all the new stone that was needed was quarried from the Bóboli gardens, where the stone for Ammannati's bridge had been cut. Twelve years after the war, the reconstructed bridge was completed.

VIA DE' TORNABUONI

MAP P.60–61, POCKET MAP A12

The shops of Via de' Tornabuoni are effectively out of bounds to those who don't travel first class. Versace, Ferragamo, Prada, Cavalli, Gucci and Armani have their outlets here: indeed, in recent years they have come to monopolize the street (and nearby Piazza Strozzi), to the dismay of many, who see further evidence of the loss of Florentine identity in the eviction of local institutions such as the Seeber bookshop, the Farmacia Inglese and the *Giacosa* café – the last of these lives on in name only, as the café of Palazzo Strozzi and as an adjunct to the huge Roberto Cavalli shop.

PALAZZO STROZZI

Piazza degli Strozzi ⓦ palazzostrozzi.org.
MAP P.60–61, POCKET MAP A11

Conspicuous wealth is nothing new on Via de' Tornabuoni. Looming above everything is the vast Palazzo Strozzi, the largest and most intimidating of all Florentine Renaissance palaces, with windows as big as gateways and embossed with lumps of stone the size of boulders. Designed by Giuliano da Sangallo, it was begun by the banker Filippo Strozzi, a figure so powerful that he was once described as "the first man of Italy", and whose family were ringleaders of the anti-Medici faction in Florence. He bought and demolished a dozen town houses to make space for this strongbox in stone, and its construction lasted from 1489 to 1536. Not until the 1930s did the Strozzi family relinquish ownership of the building, which is now administered by the Fondazione Palazzo Strozzi, under whose administration the building has become a venue for outstanding art exhibitions; it has a nice café too.

PALAZZO RUCELLAI

Via della Vigna Nuova 18. MAP P.60–61,
POCKET MAP C5

In the 1440s Giovanni Rucellai, one of the richest businessmen in the city (and an esteemed scholar too), decided to commission a new house from **Leon Battista Alberti**, whose accomplishments as architect, mathematician, linguist and theorist of the arts prompted a contemporary to exclaim, "Where shall I put Battista Alberti: in what category of learned men shall I place him?" The resultant Palazzo Rucellai, two minutes' walk from the Strozzi house at Via della Vigna Nuova 18, was the first palace in Florence to follow the rules of classical architecture; its tiers of pilasters, incised into smooth blocks of stone, evoke the exterior wall of the Colosseum. Alberti later produced another, equally elegant design for the same patron – the front of the church of Santa Maria Novella. In contrast to the feud between the Medici and the Strozzi, the Rucellai were on the closest terms with the city's *de facto* royal family: the **Loggia dei Rucellai**, across the street (now a shop), was in all likelihood

PALAZZO RUCELLAI

SANTA MARIA NOVELLA TRAIN STATION

built for the wedding of Giovanni's son to the granddaughter of Cosimo il Vecchio, and the frieze on the Palazzo Rucellai features the heraldic devices of the two families, the Medici emblem alongside the Rucellai sail.

THE MUSEO MARINO MARINI

Piazza San Pancrazio 🆆 museomarinomarini
.it. Mon & Wed–Sat 10am–5pm. €4.
MAP P.60–61, POCKET MAP A11

Round the corner from the Palazzo Rucellai stands the ex-church of San Pancrazio, deconsecrated by Napoleon, then successively the offices of the state lottery, the magistrates' court, a tobacco factory and an arsenal. It's now the swish Museo Marino Marini, a superbly designed space that holds around two hundred works left to the city in Marini's will (he died in 1980), with variations on the sculptor's trademark horse-and-rider theme – familiar from civic environments all over Europe – making up much of the show.

THE TEMPIETTO DELLO SANTO SEPOLCRO

Via della Spada. Mon–Sat 10am–noon. Free.
MAP P.60–61, POCKET MAP A11

Once part of San Pancrazio church but now entirely separate from the museum, the Cappella Rucellai, which was redesigned by Alberti, houses the marble-clad **Tempietto dello Santo Sepolcro**, the most exquisite of his architectural creations. Its form is derived from ancient Christian chapels that were themselves built in imitation of the Holy Sepulchre in Jerusalem, and its decoration is derived from Romanesque Tuscan churches such as San Miniato (see p.116). Commissioned by Giovanni Rucellai as his own funerary monument, the Tempietto was completed in 1467, more than a decade before Giovanni's death. Access to the cappella is dependent upon voluntary staff, so its opening hours are somewhat erratic.

THE TRAIN STATION

MAP P.60–61, POCKET MAP C3–C4

Most visitors barely spare a glance for **Santa Maria Novella** train station, but it's a superb building. It was in 1933 that its principal architect, Giovanni Michelucci (1891–1991), won the competition to design a new main rail terminal for the city, and its planning is so impeccably rational that it proved to be adequate for the city's needs until the start of this century.

3

WEST OF THE CENTRE

SANTA MARIA NOVELLA

Piazza Santa Maria Novella. Mon–Thurs 9am–5.30pm, Fri 11am–5.30pm, Sat 9am–5pm, Sun noon–5pm (1–5pm in winter). €5, with Museo di Santa Maria Novella. MAP P.60–61, POCKET MAP C4

The graceful church of Santa Maria Novella was the Florentine base of the Dominican order, the vigilantes of thirteenth-century Catholicism. A more humble church, Santa Maria delle Vigne, which had existed here since the eleventh century, was handed to the Dominicans in 1221; they then set about altering the place to their taste. By 1360 the interior was finished, but only the Romanesque lower part of the **facade** had been completed. This state of affairs lasted until 1456, when Giovanni Rucellai paid for Alberti to design a classical upper storey that would blend with the older section while improving the facade's proportions. The sponsor's name is picked out across the facade in Roman capitals, while the Rucellai family emblem, the billowing sail of Fortune, runs as a motif through the central frieze.

Santa Maria Novella's **interior**, which was designed to enable preachers to address their sermons to as large a congregation as possible, is adorned with a ground-breaking painting by Masaccio, a crucifix by Giotto and no fewer than three major fresco cycles. **Masaccio**'s extraordinary 1427 depiction of the **Trinity**, painted on the wall of the left aisle, was one of the earliest works in which the rules of perspective and classical proportion were rigorously employed, and Florentines queued to view the illusion on its unveiling,

stunned by a painting which appeared to create three-dimensional space on a solid wall.

Giotto's crucifix, a radically naturalistic and probably very early work (c.1288–90), hangs in what is thought to be its intended position, poised dramatically over the centre of the nave. Hitherto, it had been hidden away in the sacristy, veiled by a layer of dirt so thick that many scholars refused to recognize it as the work of the master; the attribution is still disputed by some.

The chapel to the right of the chancel is covered with a fabulous cycle of frescoes commissioned in 1489 from **Filippino Lippi** by the banker Filippo Strozzi. Illustrating the life of Strozzi's namesake, St Philip the Apostle, the paintings were commenced after Filippino had spent some time in Rome, and the work he carried out on his return displays an archeologist's obsession with ancient Roman culture. Behind the altar is Strozzi's tomb (1491–95), beautifully carved by Benedetto da Maiano.

As a chronicle of fifteenth-century life in Florence, no series of frescoes is more fascinating than **Domenico**

SANTA MARIA NOVELLA

66

THE INTERIOR OF SANTA MARIA NOVELLA

Ghirlandaio's pictures around the chancel and high altar. The artist's masterpiece, the pictures were commissioned by Giovanni Tornabuoni, a banker and uncle of Lorenzo de' Medici (Lorenzo the Magnificent), which explains why certain illustrious ladies of the Tornabuoni family are present at the births of both John the Baptist and the Virgin. These frescoes are a proud celebration of Florence at its zenith – indeed, one of the frescoes includes a Latin inscription which reads: "The year 1490, when the most beautiful city renowned for abundance, victories, arts and noble buildings profoundly enjoyed salubrity and peace." Ghirlandaio himself features in the scene in which Joachim, the Virgin's father, is chased from the temple because he has been unable to have children – the painter is the figure in the right-hand group with hand on hip.

The church's third great fresco cycle is in the **Cappella Strozzi**, which lies above the level of the rest of the church at the end of the left transept. Commissioned in 1350 as an expiation of the sin of usury by Tommaso Strozzi, an ancestor of Filippo Strozzi, the pictures are the masterpiece of Nardo di Cione, brother of the better-known Orcagna (Andrea di Cione), who painted the chapel's magnificent high altarpiece, *Christ Presenting the Keys to St Peter and the Book of Wisdom to Thomas Aquinas* (1357). Behind the altar, the central fresco depicts the *Last Judgement*, with Dante featured as one of the saved (in white, third from the left, second row from the top). So, too, are Tommaso Strozzi and his wife, shown being led by St Michael into paradise, with an angel helping the righteous up through a trapdoor; on the right of the altar, a devil forks the damned down into hell. The theme of judgement is continued in the fresco of Dante's *Inferno* on the right wall, faced by a thronged *Paradiso*.

The adjacent chapel, the Cappella Gondi, contains a crucifix carved by Brunelleschi, supposedly as a riposte to the uncouthness of Donatello's crucifix in Santa Croce.

THE MUSEO DI SANTA MARIA NOVELLA

Piazza Santa Maria Novella, but the entrance is at Piazza della Stazione 4 ⓦ museicivicifiorentini.it. Mon–Thurs 9am–5.30pm, Fri 11am–5.30pm, Sat 9am–5pm, Sun noon–5pm (1–5pm in winter). €5, with church of Santa Maria Novella. MAP P.60–61, POCKET MAP C4

Remarkable paintings are housed in the spacious Romanesque conventual buildings of Santa Maria Novella, now home to the Museo di Santa Maria Novella. The main cloister, the **Chiostro Verde**, dates from the fourteenth century and features frescoes of *Stories from Genesis* (1425–30) executed by Paolo Uccello and his workshop. The cloister takes its name from the green base *terra verde* pigment they used, and which now gives the paintings a spectral undertone. Best preserved of the frescoes is *The Flood*, a windswept scene rendered almost unintelligible by the telescoping perspective and the double appearance of the Ark (before and after the flood), whose flanks form a receding corridor in the centre of the picture.

Off the cloister opens the **Cappellone degli Spagnoli**, or Spanish Chapel, which received its present name after Eleonora di Toledo, wife of Cosimo I, reserved it for the use of her Spanish entourage. Presumably she derived much inspiration from its majestic fresco cycle (1367–69) by Andrea di Firenze, an extended depiction of the triumph of the Catholic Church that was described by Ruskin as "the most noble piece of pictorial philosophy in Italy". Virtually every patch of the walls is covered with frescoes, whose theme is the role of the Dominicans in the battle against heresy and in the salvation of Christian souls. Most spectacular is the right wall, depicting *The Triumph of the Church*. The Dominicans are of course prominent among the ranks of figures representing

The Paterenes and St Peter Martyr

In the twelfth century, Florence became the crucible of one of the reforming **religious movements** that periodically cropped up in medieval Europe. The Paterenes were convinced that everything worldly was touched by the Devil. Accordingly they despised the papacy for its claims to temporal power, and their campaign against the financial and moral corruption of the Catholic Church inevitably brought them into conflict with Rome. The displeasure of the Vatican found its means of expression in the Dominican known as St Peter Martyr. Operating from Santa Maria Novella, this papal inquisitor headed a couple of anti-Paterene fraternities, which were in effect his private army. In 1244 he led them into battle across the Piazza Santa Maria Novella, where they massacred hundreds of the theological enemy. The carnage is commemorated by the Croce al Trebbio in Via delle Belle Donne, off the eastern side of the piazza.

After this, the Dominicans turned to less militant work, founding the charitable organization called the **Misericordia**, which is still in existence today. In 1252 Peter was knifed to death, supposedly by a pair of Paterene heretics; legend relates that the dying man managed to write out the Credo with his own blood before expiring – an incident depicted in the frescoes in Santa Maria Novella's Cappellone degli Spagnoli. Within a year he'd been made a saint.

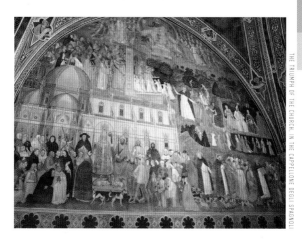

THE TRIUMPH OF THE CHURCH, IN THE CAPPELLONE DEGLI SPAGNOLI

religious orders: note St Dominic, the order's founder, unleashing the "hounds of the lord", or *Domini Canes*, a pun on the Dominicans' name. Heretics, the dogs' victims, are shown as wolves.

The contemporaneous decoration of the Chiostrino dei Morti, the oldest part of the complex, has not aged so robustly. The other cloister, the Chiostro Grande, is the property of Florence's college for the *carabinieri*, and is open to the public only on holidays.

MUSEO NAZIONALE ALINARI FOTOGRAFIA

Piazza Santa Maria Novella 14ar ⊕ mnaf.it. Mon, Tues, Thurs, Fri & Sun 10am–7.30pm. €9 (€6 on Mon). MAP P.60–61, POCKET MAP C5

The colonnaded building facing Santa Maria Novella across the piazza was formerly a hospital, which was founded back in the thirteenth century and rebuilt in the second half of the fifteenth, probably to a design by Michelozzo. Soon after its completion, Andrea della Robbia added the attractive terracotta medallions to the loggia. In the 1780s it became a crafts school for poor unmarried women, a function it retained

until the twentieth century, when it was converted into a school for children. Now, having been handsomely restored, it's home to the Museo Nazionale Alinari Fotografia. Part of the museum is set aside for one-off **photography exhibitions**, but most of the space is given over to changing displays drawn from Alinari's **archive** of more than four million pictures, covering everything from 1840s daguerre-otypes to the work of present-day photographers. The technology of the art is featured too, with a variety of cameras on show, plus stereoscopes and camera obscuras.

CHIOSTRO VERDE, MUSEO DI SANTA MARIA NOVELLA

OGNISSANTI

Borgo Ognissanti. Daily 7.30am–12.30pm & 3.30–7.30pm. Free. MAP P.68–61, POCKET MAP B5

In medieval times one of the main areas of cloth production – the mainstay of the Florentine economy – was in the west of the city. **San Salvatore in Ognissanti**, the main church of this quarter, stands on a piazza that might be taken as a symbol of the state of the present-day Florentine economy, dominated as it is by two of Florence's plushest hotels. The church was founded in 1256 by the Umiliati, a Benedictine order from Lombardy who specialized in weaving woollen cloth; in 1561 the Franciscans took over the church, the new tenure being marked by a Baroque overhaul which spared only the medieval campanile.

The young face squeezed between the Madonna and the dark-cloaked man in Ghirlandaio's *Madonna della Misericordia* (1473), over the second altar on the right, is said to be that of Amerigo Vespucci (1451–1512), an agent for the Medici in Seville, whose two voyages in 1499 and 1501 would lend his name to a continent. The altar was paid for by the Vespucci, a family of silk merchants from the Ognissanti district, which is why other members of the clan appear beneath the Madonna's cloak. Among them is Simonetta Vespucci (at the Virgin's left hand), the mistress of Giuliano de' Medici – she is said to have been the model for the face of Botticelli's Venus. The idea may not be so far-fetched, for Botticelli was born in the Ognissanti parish and lived locally, and the Vespucci and Filipepi families were on good terms. Botticelli

GIOTTO'S CRUCIFIX IN OGNISSANTI

is buried in the church, beneath a round tomb slab in the south transept (the slab bears his baptismal name, Sandro Filipepi), and his small fresco of *St Augustine's Vision of St Jerome* (1480) hangs on the same wall as the Madonna, between the third and fourth altars. Facing it is Ghirlandaio's more earthbound *St Jerome*, also painted in 1480; in the same year Ghirlandaio painted the *Last Supper* that covers one wall of the refectory, reached through the cloister entered to the left of the church (March–June Mon, Tues & Thurs–Sun 9am–5pm; rest of year Mon, Tues & Sat 9am–noon; free). And don't miss the dazzling **Crucifix** that hangs in the left transept of Ognissanti: in 2010 it emerged from a seven-year restoration, and during cleaning it was established by infrared and X-ray analysis that it's almost certainly by Giotto.

Shops

CELLERINI

Via del Sole 37r ☎ 055 282 533, Ⓦ cellerini. it. Summer Mon–Fri 9am–1pm & 3–7pm, Sat 9am–1pm; winter Mon 3–7pm, Tues–Sat 9am–1pm & 3–7pm. MAP P.60-61, POCKET MAP C5

Bags, bags and more bags, from the city's premier exponents of the craft. Their handiwork is elegant, durable and costly.

FERRAGAMO

Via de' Tornabuoni 14r ☎ 055 292 123, Ⓦ salvatoreferragamo.it. Mon–Sat 10am–7.30pm. MAP P.60-61, POCKET MAP A12

Established by Salvatore Ferragamo, once the most famous shoemaker in the world, Ferragamo now produces ready-to-wear clothing too, but the company's reputation still rests on its beautiful shoes. The shop is unbelievably grandiose, and has a museum in the basement, featuring shoes that Salvatore made for Marilyn Monroe.

IL BISONTE

Via del Parione 31–33r ☎ 055 215 722, Ⓦ ilbisonte.com. Mon–Fri 9.30am–7pm, Sat 9am–2pm. MAP P.60-61, POCKET MAP A12

Beautiful and robust bags, briefcases and accessories, many of them made from *vacchetta*, a soft cow-hide that ages very nicely.

MÜNSTERMANN

Piazza Goldoni 2r ☎ 055 210 660. Ⓦ munstermann.it. Tues–Sat 10am–1pm & 2–7pm. MAP P.60-61, POCKET MAP C5

Münstermann has been producing its own soaps and perfumes since the end of the nineteenth century, and the recipes it uses today are virtually unchanged. So if you want something a little different from the usual duty-free offerings, this is the place.

OFFICINA PROFUMO FARMACEUTICA DI SANTA MARIA NOVELLA

Via della Scala 16 ☎ 055 216 276, Ⓦ smnovella.it. Mon–Sat 9.30am–7.30pm; Sept–June also Sun 10.30am–6.30pm. MAP P.60-61, POCKET MAP C4

Occupying the pharmacy of the Santa Maria Novella monastery, this sixteenth-century shop was founded by Dominican monks as an outlet for their potions, ointments and herbal remedies. Many of these are still available, including distillations of flowers, together with face-creams and shampoos.

OTISOPSE

Via Porta Rossa 13r ☎ 055 239 6717, Ⓦ otisopse.it. Mon–Sat 9.30am–7pm. MAP P.60-61, POCKET MAP B12

Florentine footwear is of famously high quality, but can be rather staid. Otisopse, founded in Naples in 1929, goes instead for the cheap and cheerful approach – a pair of their pink desert boots or purple moccasins will cost you around €50. There are three other branches: Via de' Neri 58r (between the Signoria and Santa Croce), Via Guicciardini 2r and Piazza Nazario Sauro 17r (both Oltrarno).

OFFICINA PROFUMO FARMACEUTICA DI SANTA MARIA NOVELLA

PINEIDER

Piazza de' Rucellai 4–7r ☎ 055 284 656.
🌐 pineider.com. Mon 3–7pm, Tues–Sat 10am–7pm. MAP P.60–61, POCKET MAP C5

Pineider sells briefcases, picture frames and other accessories for home and office, but its reputation rests on its colour-coordinated calling cards, handmade papers and envelopes – as used by Napoleon, Stendhal, Byron and Shelley, to name just a few past customers.

Cafés & bars

ART BAR

Via del Moro 4r ☎ 055 287 661. Daily 7pm–midnight. MAP P.60–61, POCKET MAP C5

A fine little bar near Piazza di Carlo Goldoni. The interior looks like an antique shop, while the club-like atmosphere attracts a smart crowd. Busiest at happy hour (6.30–9pm), when the imaginative cocktails are in heavy demand.

PROCACCI

Via de' Tornabuoni 64r ☎ 055 211 656. Mon–Sat 10.30am–8pm; closed Aug. MAP P.60–61, POCKET MAP A11

This famous café doesn't serve coffee, just wine and cold drinks. Its reputation comes from the extraordinary and delicious *tartufati* (truffle-butter brioche) – from October to December.

SLOWLY

Via Porta Rossa 63r ☎ 055 264 5354.
🌐 slowlycafe.com. Daily 7pm–2.30am, plus Mon–Sat 12.30–2.30pm; closed July & Aug. MAP P.60–61, POCKET MAP B12

With its black banquettes and ice-blue lighting, *Slowly* is one of the coolest-looking bars in town, and for years it's been one of the main watering holes for Florence's style-conscious kids and young professionals. Cocktails are reassuringly expensive, but the €10 lunch buffet is a good deal. There's a DJ every night too.

Restaurants

IL CONTADINO

Via Palazzuolo 71r ☎ 055 238 2673.
🌐 trattoriailcontadino.com. Mon–Fri noon–9.30pm. MAP P.60–61, POCKET MAP B4

Small, popular place with a simple black-and-white interior and fascinating large photos of old Florence on the walls. Fast and friendly service, shared tables, and very cheap but good food. Three-course menu (with drinks) costs a mere €13.50 in the evening, and even less at lunch. No reservations.

SLOWLY

MARIONE

Via della Spada 27r ☎ 055 214 756. Daily noon–3pm & 7–10.30pm; closed first two weeks of Aug. MAP P.60–61, POCKET MAP A11

This simple old trattoria is a reliable stand-by. It's not the most refined cooking in Florence, and the ambience is brisk rather than homely, but with main courses all under €15 you can't really complain.

OLIVIERO

Via delle Terme 52r ☎ 055 212 421. ⓦ ristorante-oliviero.it. Mon–Sat 7–11pm; closed Aug. MAP P.60–61, POCKET MAP A12

Oliviero has a welcoming and old-fashioned feel – something like an Italian restaurant of the 1960s – and the menu, though predominantly Tuscan, includes dishes from other regions of Italy. Fresh fish features – something of a rarity in Florence. Expect to pay upwards of €50 per person, without wine – not unreasonable for cooking of this calibre.

OSTERIA DEI CENTO POVERI

Via Palazzuolo 31r & 41r ☎ 055 218 846. ⓦ centopoveri.it. Daily noon–3pm & 7pm–midnight. MAP P.60–61, POCKET MAP C5

This very popular *osteria* offers more fish than is customary with meat-oriented Tuscan menus, and has some excellent set menus (both fish and meat) starting at €30. Established in the 1990s, the operation has expanded in recent years, and pizzas are served at the newer branch, at 41r.

Clubs

SPACE CLUB

Via Palazzuolo 37 ☎ 055 293 082. ⓦ paceclubfirenze.com. Daily 10pm–3am. MAP P.60–61, POCKET MAP B4

Having operated for years under the name *Space Electronic*, the refurbished

Space Club is still the archetypal big Continental disco, with a karaoke area downstairs and Florence's biggest dancefloor up top.

YAB

Via de' Sassetti 5r ☎ 055 215 160, ⓦ yab.it. Mon & Wed–Sat 9pm–4am; closed June–Sept. MAP P.60–61, POCKET MAP B12

This basement club-bar-restaurant has been popular for years and is known throughout the country for Monday's "Yabsmoove" – Italy's longest-running hip-hop night. The most relaxed and reliable night's clubbing in central Florence.

Theatre & classical music

TEATRO DEL MAGGIO MUSICALE FIORENTINO

Corso Italia 16 ☎ 055 213 535. ⓦ maggiofiorentino.com. MAP P.60–61, POCKET MAP A4

Florence's main municipal theatre hosts many of the city's major classical music, dance and theatre events.

Cinemas

FULGOR

Via Maso Finiguerra 24r ☎ 055 238 1881. ⓦ planetcinema.it. MAP P.60–61, POCKET MAP B4

Central cinema with *versione originale* screenings three times a day, seven days a week.

ODEON ORIGINAL SOUND

Piazza Strozzi 2 ☎ 055 214 068. ⓦ odeonfirenze.com. Closed for part of Aug. MAP P.60–61, POCKET MAP B11

Mainstream films are screened in their original language (with Italian subtitles) at this air-conditioned cinema almost every day.

North of the centre

The San Lorenzo district, to the northwest of the Duomo, is the city's main market area, with scores of clothing and accessories stalls encircling a vast food hall. Racks of T-shirts, leather jackets and belts fill the road beside the church of San Lorenzo, a building of major importance, to which is attached another of the city's major draws, the Cappelle Medicee (Medici Chapels). While some of the most prominent members of the Medici family are buried in the main part of San Lorenzo, dozens of lesser lights are interred in these chapels, with two of them being celebrated by some of Michelangelo's finest sculptures. The Medici also account for the area's other major sight, the Palazzo Medici-Riccardi, to the north of which lies the Museo di San Marco, replete with paintings by Fra' Angelico. A brief walk from San Marco brings you to the Accademia, famous above all for Michelangelo's *David*. A short distance to the east is the graceful Piazza Santissima Annunziata, site of Brunelleschi's Spedale degli Innocenti, the superb church of Santissima Annunziata and the Museo Archeologico.

SAN LORENZO

Piazza San Lorenzo ⓦ operamedicea laurenziana.it. Mon–Sat 10am–5.30pm; March–Oct also Sun 1.30–5.30pm. €3.50, or €6 with Biblioteca Laurenziana. MAP P.76–77, POCKET MAP D4

Founded in 393, San Lorenzo has a claim to be the oldest church in Florence, and for some three hundred years it was the city's cathedral. By 1060 a sizeable Romanesque church had been built on the site, a building which in time became the Medici's parish church. In 1419 Giovanni di Bicci de' Medici, founder of the Medici fortune, offered to finance a new church, designed by **Brunelleschi**, but construction was hampered by financial problems. Giovanni's son, Cosimo de' Medici,

eventually saved the day, but his largesse was not sufficient to provide the church with a facade, a feature it still lacks.

What strikes you on stepping **inside the church** is the cool rationality of Brunelleschi's design, an instantly calming

SAGRESTIA VECCHIA, SAN LORENZO

SAN LORENZO

contrast to the hubbub outside. The first work of art to catch your attention, in the second chapel on the right, is Rosso Fiorentino's *Marriage of the Virgin* (1523), with its golden-haired and youthful Joseph. There's another arresting painting at the top of the left aisle – Bronzino's enormous fresco of *The Martyrdom of St Lawrence* (1569) – but it seems a shallow piece of work alongside the nearby bronze pulpits by Donatello. Clad with reliefs depicting scenes preceding and following the Crucifixion, these are the artist's last works (begun c.1460) and were completed by his pupils as increasing paralysis limited their master's ability to model in wax. Jagged and discomforting, charged with more energy than the space can contain, these panels are more like virtuoso sketches in bronze than conventional reliefs. Donatello is buried in the nave of the church, next to his patron, Cosimo de' Medici, and commemorated by a memorial in the chapel in the north

transept, close to Filippo Lippi's altarpiece of the *Annunciation*. Cosimo's own tomb, in the centre of the church, bears the inscription "Pater Patriae" (Father of the Fatherland) – a title once borne by Roman emperors.

Four other eminent Medici lie buried in the **Sagrestia Vecchia**, one of Brunelleschi's earliest projects (1421–26), and the only one completed in his lifetime. The space was commissioned by Giovanni Bicci de' Medici as a private chapel; on his death, Giovanni was buried beneath the massive marble slab at the centre of the chapel, with his wife, Piccarda. Another tomb, on the left as you enter, is the resting place of Giovanni's grandsons, Giovanni and Piero de' Medici. Donatello created the cherub-filled frieze and the eight tondi above it, depicting the Four Evangelists and a quartet of scenes from the life of St John; he was also responsible for the two bronze doors, showing pairs of disputatious martyrs (the left door), and the Apostles and Fathers of the Church (the right).

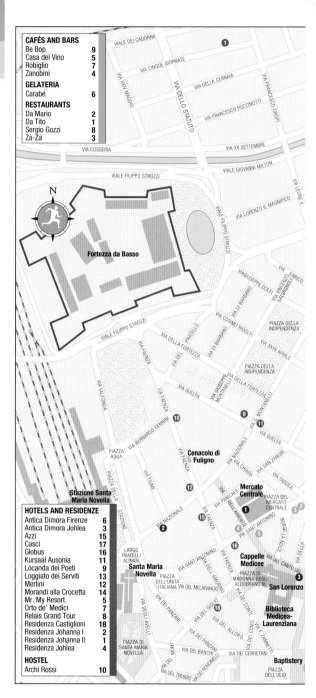

CAFÉS AND BARS
Be Bop	9
Casa del Vino	5
Robiglio	7
Zanobini	4

GELATERIA
Carabé	6

RESTAURANTS
Da Mario	2
Da Tito	1
Sergio Gozzi	8
Zà-Zà	3

HOTELS AND RESIDENZE
Antica Dimora Firenze	6
Antica Dimora Johlea	3
Azzi	15
Casci	17
Globus	16
Kursaal Ausonia	11
Locanda dei Poeti	9
Loggiato dei Serviti	13
Merlini	12
Morandi alla Crocetta	14
Mr. My Resort	5
Orto de' Medici	7
Relais Grand Tour	8
Residenza Castiglioni	18
Residenza Johanna I	2
Residenza Johanna II	1
Residenza Johlea	4

HOSTEL
Archi Rossi	10

Fortezza da Basso

Cenacolo di Fuligno

Stazione Santa Maria Novella

Mercato Centrale

Cappelle Medicee

Santa Maria Novella

San Lorenzo

Biblioteca Medicea-Laurenziana

Baptistery

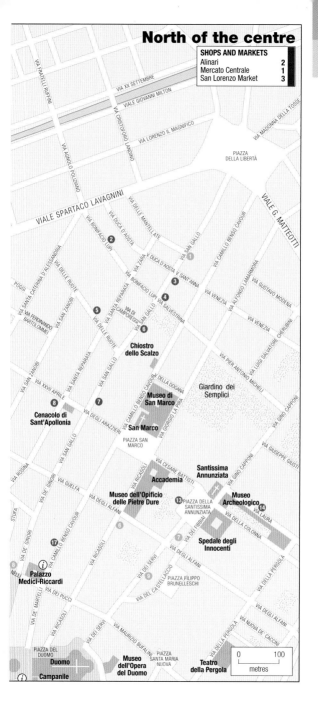

North of the centre

SHOPS AND MARKETS

Alinari	**2**
Mercato Centrale	**1**
San Lorenzo Market	**3**

THE BIBLIOTECA MEDICEA-LAURENZIANA

Piazza San Lorenzo ◐ operamedicelauren ziana.it. Mon–Sat 9.30am–1.30pm. €3, or €6 with San Lorenzo. MAP P.76–77, POCKET MAP D4

A gateway to the left of San Lorenzo leads to the Biblioteca Medicea-Laurenziana. Wishing to create a suitably grandiose home for the family's precious manuscripts, Pope Clement VII – Lorenzo's nephew – asked Michelangelo to design a new library in 1524. The **Ricetto**, or vestibule, of the building he eventually came up with (more than thirty years later) is a showpiece of Mannerist architecture, delighting in paradoxical display: brackets that support nothing, columns that sink into the walls, and a flight of steps so large that it almost fills the room.

In the reading room, too, almost everything is the work of Michelangelo, even the inlaid desks. Exhibitions in the connecting rooms draw on the 15,000-piece Medici collection, which includes manuscripts as diverse as a fifth-century copy of Virgil –

Michelangelo

Michelangelo Buonarroti (1475–1564) was born in Caprese in eastern Tuscany, but his family soon moved to Florence, where he became a pupil of Ghirlandaio, making his first stone reliefs for Lorenzo de' Medici. After the Medici were expelled from the city the young Michelangelo went to Rome in 1496. There he secured a reputation as the **most skilled sculptor** of his day with the *Bacchus* (now in the Bargello) and the *Pietà* for St Peter's.

After his return to Florence in 1501, Michelangelo carved the *David* and the *St Matthew* (both in the Accademia). He was also employed to paint a fresco of the *Battle of Cascina* in the Palazzo Vecchio. Only the cartoon was finished, but this became the single most influential work of art in the city, its twisting nudes a recurrent motif in later Mannerist art. Work was suspended in 1505 when Michelangelo was called to Rome by Pope Julius II to create his tomb; the *Slaves* in the Accademia was intended for this grandiose project which, like many of Michelangelo's schemes, was never finished.

In 1508 Michelangelo began his other superhuman project, the decoration of the **Sistine Chapel** ceiling in Rome. Back in Florence, he started work on the San Lorenzo complex in 1516, staying on to supervise its defences when it was besieged by the Medici and Charles V in 1530. Four years later he left Florence for good, and spent his last thirty years in Rome, during which he produced the *Last Judgement* in the Sistine Chapel. Florence has one work from this final phase of Michelangelo's career, the *Pietà* he intended for his own tomb (now in the Museo dell'Opera del Duomo; see p.36).

the collection's oldest item – and a treatise on architecture by Leonardo.

THE CAPPELLE MEDICEE

Piazza Madonna degli Aldobrandini
Ⓦ operamedicealaurenziana.it. Tues–Sat 8.15am–4.50pm, plus 1st, 3rd & 5th Sun of month and 2nd & 4th Mon of the month, same hours. €6. MAP P76–77, POCKET MAP D4

Michelangelo's most celebrated contribution to the San Lorenzo complex forms part of the Cappelle Medicee, which are entered from Piazza Madonna degli Aldobrandini, at the back of the church.

After passing through the crypt, where almost fifty lesser Medici are buried, you climb up to the Cappella dei Principi (Chapel of the Princes), an oppressively colourful stone-plated hall built as a mausoleum for Cosimo I and the grand dukes who succeeded him. Pass straight through for the **Sagrestia Nuova**, which was designed by Michelangelo as a tribute to Brunelleschi's Sagrestia Vecchia in the main body of San Lorenzo. The architecture plays complex games with the visual vocabulary of classical architecture, and provides a magnificent setting for the three **Medici tombs** (1520–34), two of which are wholly by Michelangelo and the other one partly.

The tomb on the left as you enter belongs to Lorenzo, Duke of Urbino, grandson of Lorenzo the Magnificent. Michelangelo depicts him as a man of thought, and his sarcophagus bears figures of *Dawn* and *Dusk*, the times of day whose ambiguities appeal to the contemplative mind. Opposite stands the tomb of Lorenzo de' Medici's youngest son, Giuliano, Duke of Nemours; as a man of action, his character is symbolized by the clear antithesis of *Day* and *Night*.

The two principal effigies were intended to face the equally grand tombs of Lorenzo de' Medici and his brother Giuliano. The only part of the project completed by Michelangelo is the *Madonna and Child*, the last image of the Madonna he ever sculpted. The figures to either side are Cosmas and Damian, patron saints of doctors (*medici*) and the Medici. Although completed by others, they follow Michelangelo's design.

THE PALAZZO MEDICI-RICCARDI

Via Cavour 1 ⓦ palazzo-medici.it. Mon,
Tues & Thurs–Sun 9am–6pm. €7. MAP P.76–77,
POCKET MAP E4

The Palazzo Medici-Riccardi
was built for Cosimo de' Medici
by Michelozzo between 1444
and 1462, and remained the
family headquarters until
Cosimo I moved to the Palazzo
Vecchio (see p.44) in 1540. In
Cosimo de Medici's prime,
around fifty members of the
clan lived here; Donatello's
Judith and Holofernes (now in
the Palazzo Vecchio) adorned
the walled garden, while the
same artist's *David* (now in the
Bargello) stood in the entrance
courtyard.

The palace now houses the
offices of the provincial
government, but you can visit
parts of it, notably the chapel
and its **cycle of frescoes**, which
a maximum of fifteen may view
at any one time. To avoid the
queues, book in advance at the
ticket office, at Via Cavour 3, or
call ⓣ 055 276 0340.

Painted around 1460,
Benozzo Gozzoli's frescoes of
The Journey of the Magi
probably portray the pageant of
the Compagnia dei Magi, the
most patrician of the city's
religious confraternities, whose
annual procession took place at
Epiphany. Several Medici were
prominent members, including
Piero de' Medici (Piero il
Gottoso), who may have
commissioned the pictures. It's
known that several of the
Medici household are featured
in the procession, but putting
names to these prettified faces
is a problem. The man leading
the cavalcade on a white horse
is almost certainly Piero.
Lorenzo il Magnifico, 11 years
old at the time the fresco was
painted, is probably the young
king in the foreground, riding
the grey horse detached from
the rest of the procession, while
his brother, Giuliano, is most
likely the one preceded by the
black bowman. The artist
himself is in the crowd on the
far left, his red beret signed
with the words "Opus Benotii"
in gold.

Another set of stairs leads up
to the **first floor**, where a
display case in the lobby of the
main gallery contains a
Madonna and Child (late
1460s) by Filippo Lippi. The
ceiling of the grandiloquent
gallery glows with Luca
Giordano's fresco of *The
Apotheosis of the Medici* (1683),
from which one can only
deduce that Giordano had no
sense of shame. Accompanying
Cosimo III on his flight into
the ether is his son, the last
male Medici, Gian Gastone,
who grew to be a man so inert
that he could rarely summon
the energy to get out of bed in
the morning.

PALAZZO MEDICI-RICCARDI

THE MERCATO CENTRALE

Piazza del Mercato Centrale (see p.90 for
market opening times). MAP P.76–77,
POCKET MAP D3

The Mercato Centrale, Europe's
largest covered **food hall**, was
designed by Giuseppe
Mengoni, architect of Milan's
famous Galleria and opened in
1874; it received a major
overhaul a century later,
reopening in 1980 with a new
upper floor. Butchers,
alimentari, tripe-sellers,
greengrocers, pasta stalls –
they're all gathered under the
one roof.

Each day from 8am to 7pm
the streets around the Mercato
Centrale are thronged with
stalls selling bags, belts, shoes,
football shirts and leather
jackets. The quality isn't the
highest, but if you fancy
practicing your haggling skills,
this is the place to do it.

THE MERCATO CENTRALE

THE CENACOLO DI FULIGNO

Via Faenza 40. Tues, Thurs & Sat 9am–noon.
Free. MAP P.76–77, POCKET MAP D3

Cenacoli (Last Suppers) were
something of a Florentine
artistic speciality, and there's a
beguiling example of the genre
– the *Cenacolo di Fuligno* – in
the former Franciscan convent
in Via Faenza. Discovered
under layers of whitewash and
grime in 1840, it was once
thought to be by Raphael, then
reassigned to Raphael's mentor
Perugino. Latest research
indicates that it was painted by
Perugino's workshop but
designed by the master in the
1490s. A small collection of
contemporaneous devotional
art hangs on the other walls of
the former refectory.

THE FORTEZZA DA BASSO

Piazza Adua. MAP P.76–77, POCKET MAP C1–C2

The Fortezza da Basso was
built to intimidate the people
of Florence by the vile
Alessandro de' Medici, who
ordained himself duke of
Florence after a ten-month
siege by the army of Charles V
and Pope Clement VII
(possibly Alessandro's father)
had forcibly restored the
Medici. Within a few years the
cruelties of Alessandro had
become intolerable; a petition
to Charles V spoke of the
Fortezza da Basso as "a prison
and a slaughterhouse for the
unhappy citizens". Charles's
response to Alessandro's atroci-
ties was to marry his daughter
to the tyrant. In the end,
another Medici came to the
rescue: in 1537 the distantly
related Lorenzaccio de' Medici
stabbed the duke to death.
Subsequently the Fortezza da
Basso fell into dereliction, but
since 1978 it has been used for
trade fairs and shows such as
the Pitti Moda fashion
jamborees in January and July;
the city's main art-restoration
workshops are here too.

THE CENACOLO DI SANT'APOLLONIA

Via XXVII Aprile 1. Daily 8.15am–1.50pm; closed 1st, 3rd & 5th Sun of month, and 2nd & 4th Mon. Free. MAP P.76–77, POCKET MAP F3

Most of the former Benedictine convent of Sant'Apollonia has now been turned into apartments, but the lower part of an entire wall of the former refectory is taken up with Andrea del Castagno's disturbing *Last Supper* (c. 1447). Blood-red is the dominant tone, and the most commanding figure is the diabolic, black-bearded Judas, who sits on the near side of the table. The seething patterns in the marbled panels behind the Apostles seem to mimic the turmoil in the mind of each as he hears Christ's announcement of the betrayal. Castagno also painted the *Crucifixion*, *Deposition* and *Resurrection* above the illusionistic space in which the Last Supper takes place, and the *Crucifixion* and *Pietà* on the adjacent walls.

THE ACCADEMIA

Via Ricasoli 66 ⓦ uffizi.firenze.it. Tues–Sun 8.15am–6.50pm. €6.50, or €11 during special exhibitions. MAP P.76–77, POCKET MAP F3

The Galleria dell'Accademia has an extensive collection of paintings, but what draws the crowds is the sculpture of **Michelangelo**, in particular the *David*. So great is the public appetite for this one work in particular that you'd be well advised to book tickets in advance (see p.147).

Commissioned by the Opera del Duomo in 1501, the **David** was conceived to invoke parallels with Florence's recent liberation from Savonarola and the Medici. It's an incomparable show of technical bravura, all the more impressive given the difficulties posed by the marble from which it was carved. The four-metre block of stone – thin, shallow and riddled with cracks – had been quarried from Carrara forty years earlier. Several artists had already attempted to work with it, notably Leonardo da Vinci. Michelangelo succeeded where others had failed, completing the work in 1504 when he was still just 29. Displayed for almost four hundred years in the Piazza della Signoria, the *David* today occupies a specially built alcove, protected by a glass barrier that was built in 1991, after one of its toes was vandalized with a hammer.

MICHELANGELO'S DAVID

SLAVES BY MICHELANGELO

commission from the Opera del Duomo; they actually requested a full series of the Apostles from Michelangelo, but this is the only one he ever began.

The **picture galleries** that flank the main sculpture hall are generally unexciting, with copious examples of the work of "Unknown Florentine" and "Follower of …". The pieces likeliest to make an impact are Pontormo's *Venus and Cupid* (1532), painted to a cartoon by Michelangelo; a *Madonna of the Sea* (1470) attributed to Botticelli; and the painted fifteenth-century *Adimari Chest*, showing a Florentine wedding ceremony in the Piazza del Duomo.

THE MUSEO DELL'OPIFICIO DELLE PIETRE DURE

Via degli Alfani 78. Mon–Sat 8.15am–2pm. €4. MAP P.76–77, POCKET MAP F3

Occupying a corner of the Accademia building, the Opificio delle Pietre Dure was founded in 1588 to train craftsmen in the distinctively Florentine art of creating pictures or patterns with highly polished, inlaid **semi-precious stones**. The museum clearly elucidates the highly skilled processes involved in the creation of *pietre dure* work, and has some remarkable examples of the genre. If you want to see some more spectacular (and rather gross) specimens, you should visit the Cappelle Medicee (see p.79) or the Palazzo Pitti's Museo degli Argenti. While local workshops still maintain the traditions of this specialized art-form, the Opificio itself has evolved into one of the world's leading centres for the restoration of stonework.

In 2004 he was given a thorough cleaning for the first time in decades, restoring the gangly youth to something like his original brilliance.

Michelangelo once described the process of carving as being the liberation of the form from within the stone, a notion that seems to be embodied by the unfinished **Slaves** (or Prisoners). His procedure, clearly demonstrated here, was to cut the figure as if it were a deep relief, and then to free the three-dimensional figure; often his assistants would perform the initial operation, so it's possible that Michelangelo's own chisel never actually touched these stones. Probably carved in the late 1520s, the statues were originally destined for the tomb of Julius II, a project that was eventually abandoned; four of the original six statues came to the Accademia in 1909, while two others found their way to the Louvre.

Close by is another unfinished work, *St Matthew* (1505–06), started soon after completion of the *David* as a

THE MUSEO DI SAN MARCO

Piazza San Marco ⓦ uffizi.firenze.it. Tues–Fri 8.15am–1.50pm, Sat 8.15am–4.50pm, plus 1st, 3rd & 5th Mon of the month 8.15am–1.50pm, and 2nd & 4th Sun of the month 8.15am–4.50pm. €4. MAP P.76–77, POCKET MAP F3

Much of the north side of Piazza San Marco is taken up by the Dominican convent of San Marco, now the home of the Museo di San Marco. The Dominicans acquired the site in 1436, and the complex promptly became the recipient of Cosimo de' Medici's most lavish patronage. Ironically, the convent became the centre of resistance to the Medici later in the century: Girolamo Savonarola, leader of the government of Florence after the expulsion of the Medici in 1494, was the prior of San Marco.

During the Medici-funded rebuilding, the convent was decorated by one of its friars and a future prior, Fra' Angelico, a Tuscan painter in whom a medieval simplicity of faith was uniquely allied to a Renaissance sophistication of manner. Twenty or so paintings by the artist are gathered in the ground-floor **Ospizio dei Pellegrini**, or Pilgrims' Hospice, including several of Angelico's most famous creations. Here you'll see a wonderful

Deposition that originally hung in the church of Santa Trìnita, the *Madonna dei Linaiuoli* (1433), which was Angelico's first major public painting, and the so-called *Pala di San Marco* (1440), a painting that has been badly damaged by the passage of time and a disastrous restoration, but demonstrates Fra' Angelico's familiarity with the principle of a central vanishing point, as expounded in Alberti's *Della Pittura* (*On Painting*), published in Italian just two years before the picture was executed.

Elsewhere on ground level you'll find Fra' Bartolomeo's portrait of Savonarola, his unfinished *Pala della Signoria*, and – in the **Sala Capitolare**, or Chapter House – a powerful fresco of the *Crucifixion*, painted by Angelico and assistants. Most of the main cloister's frescoes are sixteenth-century depictions of episodes from the life of Antonino Pierozzi, Fra' Angelico's mentor, who was canonized as St Antonine in 1523; Fra' Angelico himself painted the frescoes in its four corners. Before going upstairs, make sure you also see the **Refettorio Piccolo**, or Small Refectory, which has a lustrous *Last Supper* (1480) by Ghirlandaio.

FRA' ANGELICO FRESCO, SAN MARCO

MAIN CLOISTER, SAN MARCO

At the top of the stairs you're confronted with one of the most sublime paintings in Italy: for the drama of its setting and the lucidity of its composition, nothing in San Marco matches Angelico's *Annunciation*. Angelico and his assistants also painted the simple and piously restrained pictures in each of the 44 **dormitory cells** on this floor, into which the friars would withdraw for solitary contemplation and sleep. Several of the scenes include one or both of a pair of monastic onlookers, serving as intermediaries between the occupant of the cell and the personages in the pictures: the one with the star above his head is St Dominic; the one with the split skull is St Peter Martyr.

The rooms once occupied by Savonarola now contain various relics questionably authenti-cated as worn by the man himself; the more luxuriously appointed cells 29 and 30 were the personal domain of Cosimo de' Medici – the fresco of the *Adoration of the Magi* may have been suggested by Cosimo himself, who liked to think of himself as a latter-day wise man and gift-giving king.

On the way to these VIP cells you'll pass the entrance to **Michelozzo's Library**, built in 1441–44 to a design that exudes an atmosphere of calm study. Cosimo's agents roamed as far as the Near East garnering precious manuscripts and books for him; in turn, Cosimo handed all the religious items over to the monastery, stipulating that they should be accessible to all, making this Europe's first **public library**. As the plaque by the doorway tells you, it was on this spot that Savonarola was arrested in 1498.

SAN MARCO CHURCH

Piazza San Marco. Mon–Sat 9.30am–noon & 4–5.30pm. Free. MAP P.76–77, POCKET MAP F3

The church of San Marco is worth a quick visit for two works on the second and third altars on the right: a *Madonna and Saints* painted in 1509 by Fra' Bartolomeo, and an eighth-century mosaic of *The Madonna in Prayer* (surrounded by later additions), brought here from Rome. This had to be cut in half in transit, and you can still see the break across the Virgin's midriff. The preserved body of St Antonine lies in a chapel designed by Giambo-logna, and the great Renaissance humanists Pico della Mirandola and Poliziano are entombed in the left wall of the nave, above the statue of Savonarola.

THE CHIOSTRO DELLO SCALZO

Via Cavour 69. Mon, Thurs & Sat 8.15am–1.50pm. Free. MAP P.76–77, POCKET MAP E2

Lo Scalzo was the home of the **Brotherhood of St John**, whose vows of poverty entailed walking around barefoot (*scalzo*). The order was suppressed in 1785 and their monastery sold off, except for the cloister, which was the training ground for Andrea del Sarto; his monochrome paintings of *The Cardinal Virtues* and *Scenes from the Life of the Baptist* occupied him off and on for a decade from 1511. A couple of the sixteen scenes – *John in the Wilderness* and *John meeting Christ* – were executed by his pupil Franciabigio in 1518, when del Sarto was away in Paris.

THE GIARDINO DEI SEMPLICI

Via La Pira. April to mid-Oct Mon, Tues & Thurs–Sun 10am–7pm; rest of year Mon, Sat & Sun 10am–5pm. €6. MAP P.76–77, POCKET MAP F3

The Giardino dei Semplici or Orto Botanico – the nearest

THE GIARDINO DEI SEMPLICI

equivalent to the Bóboli garden on the north side of the city – was set up in 1545 for Cosimo I as a **medicinal garden**, following the examples of Padua and Pisa, and now covers five acres, most of the area being taken up by the original flowerbeds and avenues. The **university museums** that adjoin the Giardino dei Semplici – the Museo Botanico, the Museo di Minerologia e Litologia and the Museo di Geologia e Paleontologia – are of specialist interest.

PIAZZA SANTISSIMA ANNUNZIATA

MAP P.76–77, POCKET MAP F3–F4

Nineteenth-century urban renewal schemes left many of Florence's squares rather grim places, which makes the pedestrianized Piazza Santissima Annunziata, with its distinctive **arcades**, all the more attractive a public space. It has a special importance for the city, too. Until the end of the eighteenth century the Florentine year used to begin on March 25, the Festival of the Annunciation – hence the Florentine predilection for paintings of the Annunciation, and the fashionableness of the Annunziata church, which has long been the place for big weddings. The festival is still marked by a huge fair in the piazza and the streets leading off it; later in the year, on the first weekend in September, the square is used for Tuscany's largest crafts fair.

Brunelleschi began the piazza in the 1420s, with additions made later by Ammannati and Antonio da Sangallo. The equestrian statue of Grand Duke Ferdinando I (1608) at its centre was

ONE OF TACCA'S FOUNTAINS, PIAZZA SANTISSIMA ANNUNZIATA

the new classically influenced style. (The building on the other side of the piazza was designed a century later, by Antonio da Sangallo and Baccio d'Agnolo, as accommodation for the Servite friars who staffed the orphanage.) Andrea della Robbia's blue-backed ceramic tondi of well-swaddled babies advertise the building's function, but their gaiety belies the misery associated with it. Slavery was part of the Florentine economy as late as the fifteenth century (it's probable that Leonardo da Vinci's mother was a slave), and many of the infants given to the care of the Spedale were born to domestic slaves. From 1660 children could be abandoned anonymously in the *rota*, a small revolving door whose bricked-up remains are still visible at the extreme left of the facade; it remained in use until 1875.

The building within centres on two beautiful **cloisters**, Brunelleschi's central Chiostro degli Uomini (Men's Cloister) and the narrow, graceful Chiostro delle Donne (Women's Cloister) to the right. (These can be visited throughout the day, free of charge.) Stairs from the left-hand corner of the former lead up to the museum, a miscellany of Florentine Renaissance art that includes one of Luca della Robbia's most beguiling Madonnas and an *Adoration of the Magi* (1488) by Domenico Ghirlandaio. The latter, commissioned as the altarpiece of the building's church, features a background depicting the *Massacre of the Innocents*. The parallel of the slaughter of Bethlehem's first-born with the orphanage's foundlings, or *innocenti*, was deliberately made.

Giambologna's final work, and was cast by his pupil Pietro Tacca, from cannons captured at the Battle of Lepanto. Tacca was also the creator of the two bizarre **fountains**, on each of which a pair of aquatic monkeys spit water at two whiskered sea slugs.

THE SPEDALE DEGLI INNOCENTI

Piazza Santissima Annunziata ⓦwww
.istitutodeglinnocenti.it. Mon–Sat 10am–7pm,
Sun 8.30am–2pm. €5. MAP P.76–77.
POCKET MAP F4

Piazza Santissima Annunziata's most elegant building is the Spedale degli Innocenti, or Ospedale. Commissioned in 1419 by the Arte della Seta, the silk-weavers' guild, it opened in 1445 as the first foundlings' hospital in Europe, and is still an **orphanage** today. It was largely designed by Brunelleschi, and his nine-arched loggia was one of Europe's earliest examples of

SANTISSIMA ANNUNZIATA

Piazza Santissima Annunziata. Daily 7.30am–12.30pm & 4–6.30pm, plus Sun 8.45–9.45pm. Free. MAP P.76–77, POCKET MAP F3

Santissima Annunziata is the mother church of the **Servites**, or Servi di Maria (Servants of Mary), a religious order founded by Filippo Benizzi and six Florentine aristocrats in 1234. From humble beginnings, the order blossomed after 1252, when a painting of the Virgin begun by one of the monks but abandoned in despair because of his inability to create a truly beautiful image, was supposedly completed by an angel while he slept. So many people came to venerate the image that by 1444 a new church, financed by the Medici, was commissioned from Michelozzo, who happened to be the brother of the Servites' head prior.

As the number of pilgrims to the church increased, so it became a custom to leave wax votive offerings (*voti*) in honour of its miraculous Madonna. These became so numerous that in 1447 a special atrium, the **Chiostrino dei Voti**, was built onto the church, and in 1516 a major fresco cycle was commissioned, on the occasion of the canonization of Filippo Benizzi. Three leading artists of the day, Andrea del Sarto, Jacopo Pontormo and Rosso Fiorentino, were involved, together with several lesser painters. Some of the panels are in a poor state – all were removed from the walls and restored after the 1966 flood (see box, p.98) – but their overall effect is superb.

Just inside the church itself, on the left, stands the ornate tabernacle (1448–61) designed by Michelozzo to house the miraculous image of the Madonna. The nearby **Cappella Feroni** features a fresco by Andrea del Castagno of *Christ and St Julian* (1455–56); a more striking fresco by the same artist, *The Holy Trinity and St Jerome* (1454), can be seen in the adjacent chapel. Now restored, both frescoes were obliterated after Vasari spread the rumour that Castagno had poisoned his erstwhile friend, Domenico Veneziano, motivated by envy of the other's skill with oil paint. Castagno was saddled with this crime until the nineteenth century, when an archivist discovered that the alleged murderer in fact predeceased his victim by four years. The church's other notable painting is Andrea del Sarto's intimate *Madonna del Sacco* (1525) in the spacious **Chiostro dei Morti**, over the door that opens from the north transept (you may need to find the sacristan to open it); the picture – more formally known as *Rest during the Flight into Egypt* – takes its curious name from the sack on which St Joseph is leaning.

SANTISSIMA ANNUNZIATA

THE MUSEO ARCHEOLOGICO

Via della Colonna 36 ⓦ firenzemusei.it.
Tues–Fri 8.30am–7pm, Sat & Sun
8.30am–2pm. €4. MAP P.76–77, POCKET MAP F3–G4

The special strength of the
Museo Archeologico is its
Etruscan collection, much of it
bequeathed, inevitably, by the
Medici. Most of the finds are
on the first floor, where there's
a large array of funerary figures
and two outstanding bronze
sculptures: the *Arringatore*
(Orator), the only known large
Etruscan bronze from the
Hellenistic period, made some
time around 100 BC; and the
Chimera, a triple-headed
monster made in the fourth
century BC.

Numerous dowdy cabinets
are stuffed with unlabelled
Etruscan figurines, and much
of the **Egyptian collection** is
displayed in a similarly
uninspiring manner. The single
most remarkable object amid
the assembly of papyri,
statuettes and mummy cases is
a Hittite chariot made of bone
and wood, dating from the
fourteenth century BC.

There are more Etruscan
pieces on the top floor
(sometimes open only to
guided tours), but here the
primary focus is on the
Greek and Roman collections.
The star piece in the huge
hoard of Greek vases is the
large *François Vase*, a
sixth-century BC *krater*.
Another attention-grabbing
item is the life-size bronze
torso known as the *Torso di
Livorno*, either a fifth-century
BC Greek original or a Roman
copy. There's some debate also
about the large horse's head
that's on show in the same
room. This fragment of a
full-size statue is probably an
early Hellenistic bronze from
around 100 BC, but again it
may be a Roman copy; what's
known for certain is that it was
once in the garden of the
Palazzo Medici, where it was
studied by Donatello and
Verrocchio. Also on this floor
you'll see two beautiful
sixth-century BC Greek *kouroi*,
dubbed *Apollo* and *Apollino*,
and the bronze statue of a
young man known as the
Idolino di Pésaro – it's generally
thought to be a Roman replica
of a Greek figure dating from
around 100 BC.

THE CHIMERA IN THE MUSEO ARCHEOLOGICO

Shops & markets

ALINARI

Largo Alinari 15 ☎ 055 239 51. Ⓦ alinari.it.
Mon–Fri 9am–1pm & 2–6pm; closed 2 weeks
in mid-Aug. MAP P.76-77, POCKET MAP D4

Established in 1852, this is the
world's oldest photographic
business. Owners of the best
archive of vintage photographs
in Italy, they will print any
image you choose from their
huge catalogue. They also
publish books, calendars,
posters and cards.

MERCATO CENTRALE

Piazza del Mercato Centrale. Mon–Sat
7am–2pm; winter also Sat 4–8pm. MAP P.76-77,
POCKET MAP D3

The vast food hall is great for
picnic supplies, but well worth
a sightseeing and people-
watching visit whether you
intend to buy anything or not.
Nerbone, the market's excellent
tavola calda, serves meatballs,
pasta, stews, soups, salads and
sandwiches – perfect for a
simple but hearty lunch.

SAN LORENZO MARKET

Piazza di San Lorenzo. Daily 9am–7pm.
MAP P.76-77, POCKET MAP E4

A huge open-air warehouse of
cheap clothing, as well-organized

as a shopping mall: huge
waterproof awnings ensure that
the weather can't stop the
trading.

Cafés & bars

BE BOP

Via dei Servi 76r ☎ 055 490 397. Tues–Sun
7pm–3am. MAP P.76-77, POCKET MAP F4

A nice rock, jazz and blues bar,
with faux Art Nouveau decor.
Located close to the university
district, and often full of
students as a result. There's no
dancefloor as such; this is more
a place to sit and chill out to
the music.

CASA DEL VINO

Via dell'Ariento 16r ☎ 055 215 609. Oct–May
Mon–Sat 9.30am–5pm; June, July & Sept
closed Sat; closed all Aug. MAP P.76-77,
POCKET MAP D4

Located a few yards from the
Mercato Centrale, this wine bar
is thronged at lunchtime with
traders who pitch up for a
drink, a chat with owner
Gianni Migliorini and a few
panini or *crostini*.

ROBIGLIO

Via dei Servi 112r ☎ 055 214 501. Mon–Sat
8am–8pm. MAP P.76-77, POCKET MAP F4

Renowned for its pastries and
chocolates, *Robiglio* also makes
good ice cream and specializes
in a hot chocolate drink that's so
thick it's barely a liquid.
Founded here in 1928, *Robiglio*
now has four other branches, the
most central of which is at Via
Tosinghi 11r, near the Duomo.

ZANOBINI

Via Sant'Antonino 47r ☎ 055 239 6850.
Mon–Sat 8am–2pm & 3.30–8pm. MAP P.76-77,
POCKET MAP D4

Like the nearby *Casa del Vino*
this is an authentic and
long-established place, but here
the emphasis is more on the

HANDBAGS FOR SALE, SAN LORENZO MARKET

ROBIGLIO

wine: few bars in Florence have a better selection.

Gelateria

CARABÉ

Via Ricasoli 60r ☎ 055 289 476. April–Oct daily 10am–1am; Nov–March 11am–8pm, but closed mid-Dec to mid-Jan. MAP P.76–77, POCKET MAP E4

Wonderful Sicilian ice cream made with Sicilian ingredients as only they know how. Try the *Spirito Siciliano* flavour – the most lemony lemon you'll ever taste. Also serves delicious *cannoli* (pastry stuffed with sweet ricotta and candied fruits).

Restaurants

DA MARIO

Via Rosina 2r ☎ 055 218 550, ⓦ trattoria -mario.com. Mon–Sat noon–3.30pm; closed Aug. MAP P.76–77, POCKET MAP E3

For earthy Florentine cooking at very low prices, there's nowhere better than *Da Mario*, which has been in operation since 1953. It's just a pity it isn't open in the evenings. No credit cards; no booking.

DA TITO

Via San Gallo 112r ☎ 055 472 475. Mon–Sat 12.30–3pm & 7–11pm, Sun 7–11pm. MAP P.76–77, POCKET MAP F2

Full of locals every night and offering excellent food at fair prices (*secondi* €10–15), *Da Tito* is well worth the extra few minutes' walk from the centre. But if you don't like your meat the way Florentines like it, go elsewhere – they refuse to serve anything "well done".

SERGIO GOZZI

Piazza San Lorenzo 8r ☎ 055 281 941. Mon–Sat 10am–4pm. MAP P.76–77, POCKET MAP E4

This plain bar-trattoria, lurking behind the San Lorenzo market stalls, is a good choice for an inexpensive lunch, with a short and simple menu that changes daily. Like the rather similar *Da Mario* (see above), it does not take reservations.

ZÀ-ZÀ

Piazza del Mercato Centrale 26r ☎ 055 215 411. ⓦ trattoriazaza.it. Daily noon–3pm & 7pm–1am. MAP P.76–77, POCKET MAP E3

In business for thirty years, *Zà-Zà* has become so popular that booking is virtually obligatory in summer. The interior is dark, stone-walled and brick-arched, but in summer there are more tables on an outside terrace. There's usually a set-price menu for around €20; otherwise you'll pay around €30 per head.

East of the centre

The vast Franciscan church of Santa Croce is one of the most compelling sights in Florence, and forms the centrepiece of an area which, prior to the terrible flood of 1966, was one of the city's more densely populated districts. When the Arno burst its banks, this low-lying quarter, packed with tenements and small workshops, was virtually wrecked, and many of its residents moved out permanently in the following years. Now, however, the district has revived in a big way, and it's here that you'll find many of the city's liveliest bars and best restaurants. In addition to the mighty Santa Croce, the district's cultural attractions are the Museo Horne, the Casa Buonarroti, and a brace of smaller churches.

SANTA CROCE

Piazza Santa Croce ⓦ santacroceopera.it. Mon–Sat 9.30am–5.30pm, Sun 1–5.30pm. €6, or €8.50 combined ticket with Casa Buonarroti (see p.94). MAP P.94–95. POCKET MAP F6–G6

The church of Santa Croce is the Franciscans' principal church in Florence and is said to have been founded by St Francis himself. In truth it was probably begun seventy or so years after Francis's death, in 1294, possibly by the architect of the Duomo, Arnolfo di Cambio. Ironically, it was the city's richest families who funded the construction of the church: plutocrats such as the Bardi, Peruzzi and Baroncelli sponsored the extraordinary **fresco cycles** that were lavished on the chapels over the years, particularly during the fourteenth century, when artists of the stature of Giotto and the Gaddi family worked here. And Santa Croce has long served as the national pantheon: it contains monuments to more than 270 illustrious Italians, including

PRIMO CHIOSTRO, SANTA CROCE

SANTA CROCE

of the pictures onto dry plaster, but the vandalism of later generations was far more destructive. Scenes from the lives of St John the Evangelist and St John the Baptist fill the Peruzzi chapel, while a better-preserved cycle of the life of St Francis fills the Bardi. Despite the areas of paint destroyed when a tomb was attached to the wall, the *Funeral of St Francis* is still a composition of extraordinary impact, the grief-stricken mourners suggesting an affinity with the lamentation over the body of Christ – one of them even probes the wound in Francis's side, echoing the gesture of Doubting Thomas.

On the other side of the church there's a second **Cappella Bardi**, which houses a wooden crucifix by Donatello, supposedly criticized by Brunelleschi as resembling a "peasant on the Cross".

The door in the right aisle leads through into the church's Primo Chiostro (First Cloister), site of Brunelleschi's **Cappella Pazzi**, the epitome of the learned, harmonious spirit of early Renaissance architecture, with lovely terracotta work by Luca della Robbia and his workshop.

The **Museo dell'Opera di Santa Croce**, flanking the first cloister, houses a miscellany of art works, the most famous of which is Cimabue's flood-damaged Crucifix. Other highlights include a detached fresco of the *Last Supper* (1333), which is the earliest surviving example of the many Last Suppers (*cenacoli*) dotted around the city, and Donatello's enormous gilded *St Louis of Toulouse* (1424). Adjoining the museum is the spacious and serene **Inner Cloister,** another late project by Brunelleschi.

Michelangelo, Galileo, Machiavelli and Dante (though the last is not buried here).

On your way to the frescoed chapels be sure to take a look at Donatello's gilded stone relief of the *Annunciation* (against the right-hand wall) and Bernardo Rossellino's nearby tomb of Leonardo Bruni, chancellor of the Republic, humanist scholar and author of the first history of the city. (His successor as chancellor, Carlo Marsuppini, is commemorated by a splendid tomb in the opposite aisle, carved by Desiderio da Settignano.) The **Cappella Castellani**, at the end of the south aisle, was strikingly frescoed by Agnolo Gaddi and his pupils, while the adjoining **Cappella Baroncelli** was decorated by Agnolo's father, Taddeo, a long-time assistant to Giotto.

Both the **Cappella Peruzzi** and the **Cappella Bardi** – the two chapels on the right of the chancel – are covered with frescoes by Giotto, with some assistance in the latter. Their deterioration was partly caused by Giotto's having painted some

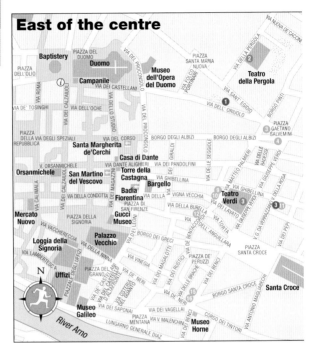

East of the centre

CASA BUONARROTI

Via Ghibellina 70 casabuonarroti.it. Mon & Wed–Sun 10am–5pm. €6.50 or €8.50 combined ticket with Santa Croce (see p.92). MAP P.94–95, POCKET MAP G6

The enticing name of the Casa Buonarroti is somewhat misleading: **Michelangelo Buonarroti** certainly owned three houses here in 1508, and probably lived on the site intermittently between 1516 and 1525, but little trace of the earlier houses remains. Today the house contains a smart but low-key **museum**, nicely decorated in period style and adorned with beautiful furniture, objets d'art, frescoed ceilings and the like, but only a handful of the works of art on display are by Michelangelo. The *Madonna della Scala* (c.1490–92) is Michelangelo's earliest known work, a delicate relief carved when he was no

older than 16. The similarly unfinished *Battle of the Centaurs* was created shortly afterwards, when he was living in the Medici household. In the adjacent room you'll find the artist's wooden model (1517) for the facade of San Lorenzo, close to the largest of all the sculptural models on display, the torso of a *River God* (1524), a work probably intended for the Medici chapel in San Lorenzo. Other rooms contain small and fragmentary pieces, possibly by the master, possibly copies of works by him.

SANT'AMBROGIO

Piazza di Sant'Ambrogio. Daily 8am–12.30pm & 4–7pm. Free. MAP P.94–95, POCKET MAP H5

Sant'Ambrogio is one of Florence's oldest churches, having been documented in 988, though rebuilding over the centuries has resulted in a

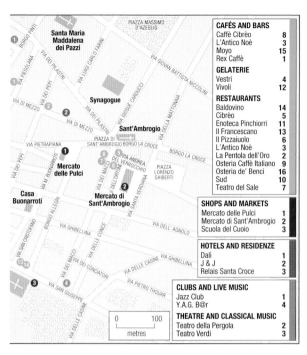

somewhat bland appearance. Inside you'll find a *Madonna Enthroned with SS John the Baptist and Bartholomew* (second altar on the right), attributed to Orcagna (or the school of Orcagna), and a recently restored triptych in the chapel to the right of the main altar, attributed to Lorenzo di Bicci or Bicci di Lorenzo. More compelling than either painting, though, is the **Cappella del Miracolo**, the chapel to the left of the high altar, and its tabernacle (1481–83) by Mino da Fiesole, an accomplished sculptor whose name crops up time and again across Tuscany. This was one of Mino's last works – he died in 1484 – making it fitting that he should be buried close by, in a pavement tomb at the chapel entrance. (Another great artist, Verrocchio, who died in

1488, is buried in the fourth chapel.)

The narrative fresco (1486) alongside the tabernacle alludes to the miracle which gave the Cappella del Miracolo its name. The work of Cosimo Rosselli (best known for his frescoes in Santissima Annunziata), it depicts a procession bearing a chalice in which, during a Mass conducted here in 1230, the communion wine was discovered to have turned into blood. The Florentines believed the chalice saved them from, among other things, the effects of a plague outbreak of 1340. The painting is full of portraits of Rosselli's contemporaries, making it another of Florence's vivid pieces of Renaissance social reportage: Rosselli himself is the figure in the black beret at the extreme left of the picture.

THE SYNAGOGUE

Via Farini 4. April–Sept Sun–Thurs
10am–6pm, Fri 10am–2pm; Oct–March
Sun–Thurs 10am–3pm, Fri 10am–2pm. €5.
MAP P.94–95, POCKET MAP G5

The enormous domed building
rising to the north of
Sant'Ambrogio church is the
Synagogue; the ghetto
established in this district by
Cosimo I was not demolished
until the second half of the
nineteenth century, which is
when the present Moorish-style
synagogue was built. It contains
a **museum** that charts the
history of Florence's Jewish
population.

SANTA MARIA MADDALENA DEI PAZZI

Borgo Pinti. Church Mon–Sat 8am–12.30pm
& 4–7pm, Sun 8am–12.30pm. Perugino
fresco Tues & Thurs 2.30–5.30pm. Free.
MAP P.94–95, POCKET MAP G4

The church of Santa Maria
Maddalena dei Pazzi is named
named after a Carmelite nun –
a member of the clan who
murdered Giuliano de' Medici
(see p.34) – who was famed
for her healing powers and
religious ecstasies: when
possessed by the spirit she
would spew words at such a
rate that a team of eight
novices was needed to
transcribe her inspired
dictation. She was also prone
to pouring boiling wax over
her arms, and was fond of
reclining naked on a bed of
thorns. Such fervent piety was
much honoured in Counter-
Reformation Florence, and a
cult grew up around her
immediately after her death in
1607; canonisation followed in
1669.

Founded in the thirteenth
century, the church is fronted
by a lovely courtyard designed
by Giuliano da Sangallo. Inside,
paintings celebrating

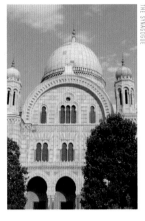

THE SYNAGOGUE

St Maria – including a pair by
Luca Giordano – adorn the
marble-clad chancel. In
contrast to all this Baroque
fervour, the convent's
chapterhouse – entered via a
doorway at Via della Colonna 9
– is decorated with a radiant
Perugino fresco of the
Crucifixion. Based on the
terrain around Lago Trasimeno,
the scene is painted as a
continuous panorama on a wall
divided into three arches,
giving the effect of looking out
through a loggia onto a
springtime landscape. As
always with Perugino, there is
nothing troubling here, the
Crucifixion being depicted not
as an agonizing death but
rather as the necessary prelude
to the Resurrection.

THE ENGLISH CEMETERY

Piazza Donatello. Daily 9am–noon & 3–6pm.
MAP P.94–95, POCKET MAP H3

North of the Pazzi church, at
the end of Borgo Pinti, lies the
English Cemetery. Now
stranded amid the traffic, this
patch of garden is the resting
place of Elizabeth Barrett
Browning and a number of
contemporaneous artistic Brits,
among them Walter Savage

Landor and Arthur Hugh Clough.

THE MUSEO HORNE

Via de' Benci 6 ⓦ www.museohorne.it. Mon–Sat 9am–1pm. €6. MAP P.94–95, POCKET MAP F7

The Museo della Fondazione Horne is one of Florence's more esoteric museums. Its collection was left to the state by the English art historian Herbert Percy Horne (1864–1916), who was instrumental in rescuing Botticelli from neglect with a pioneering biography that was published in 1908. The half-dozen rooms of paintings, sculptures, pottery, furniture and other domestic objects contain few masterpieces, but are diverting enough if you've already done the major collections.

The museum building, the **Palazzo Corsi-Alberti** (1489), is worth a look even if you're not going into the museum. Commissioned by the Corsi family, it's a typical merchant's house of the period, with huge cellars in which wool would have been dyed, and an open gallery above the courtyard for drying the finished cloth.

The pride of Horne's collection was its drawings, which are now salted away in the Uffizi, though a small display is maintained in the room on the right of the ground floor. On the first floor, the highlight of Room 1 is a tiny and badly damaged panel (once part of a triptych) by Masaccio, showing *Scenes from the Life of St Julian*; nearby there's an unfinished and age-darkened *Deposition* by Gozzoli, his last documented work. The next room contains the collection's big draw, Giotto's *St Stephen* (a fragment from a polyptych), which was probably painted at around the time Giotto was at work in Santa Croce. Room 3 has a tondo of the *Holy Family* by Beccafumi, who is also attributed with a *Drunkenness of Noah* on the second floor, where you'll also find minor works by Filippo and Filippino Lippi. One of the main exhibits on this storey is a piece of little artistic merit but great historical interest: a copy of part of Leonardo's *Battle of Anghiari*, once frescoed on a wall of the Palazzo Vecchio.

SANT'AMBROGIO

Florence's floods

Calamitous floods are nothing new in Florence. Great areas of the city were destroyed by floodwater in 1178, and in 1269 the Carraia and Trìnita bridges were carried away on a torrent so heavy that "a great part of the city of Florence became a lake", as a contemporary chronicler put it. Bridges were also destroyed by the raging Arno in 1333, and Cosimo I instituted an urban beautification scheme after a flood put nearly twenty feet of muddy water over parts of the city in 1557; on that occasion the Trìnita bridge was hit so suddenly that everyone on it was drowned, except for a couple of children who were left stranded on a pillar in midstream, where for two days they were fed by means of a rope slung over from the bank.

It rained continuously for forty days prior to November 4, **1966**, with nearly half a metre of rain falling in the preceding two days. When the water pressure in an upstream reservoir threatened to break the dam, it was decided to open the sluices. The only people to be warned about the rapidly rising level of the river were the jewellers of the Ponte Vecchio, whose private nightwatchman phoned them in the small hours of the morning with news that the bridge was starting to shake. When the banks of the Arno finally broke, a flash flood dumped around 500,000 tonnes of water and mud on the streets, moving with such speed that people were drowned in the underpass of Santa Maria Novella train station. In all, 35 Florentines were killed, 6000 shops put out of business, more than 10,000 homes made uninhabitable, some 15,000 cars wrecked, and thousands of works of art damaged, many of them ruined by heating oil flushed out of basements.

Within hours an impromptu army of rescue workers had been formed to haul pictures out of slime-filled churches and gather fragments of paint in plastic bags. Donations came in from all over the world, but the task was so immense that the restoration of many items is still continuing – scores of precious books from the National Library, which is located next door to Santa Croce and took the brunt of the flood, remain in the laboratories. In total around two-thirds of the 3000 paintings damaged in the flood are now on view again (including the great **Cimabue Crucifix**, pictured, which has become an emblem of the disaster), and two laboratories – one for paintings and one for stonework – are operating full time in Florence, developing restoration techniques that are taken up by galleries all over the world. Today, throughout the city, you can see small marble plaques with a red line showing the level the floodwaters reached on that dreadful day in 1966.

Shops & markets

MERCATO DELLE PULCI

Piazza dei Ciompi. Summer Mon–Sat 10am–1pm & 4–7pm; winter Mon–Sat 9am–1pm & 3–7pm; also open same hours on last Sun of month. MAP P.94–95, POCKET MAP G5

Much of the stuff on sale at the Mercato delle Pulci or Flea Market is overpriced junk, though you can find a few interesting items at modest cost – old postcards, posters and so on. Vasari's Loggia del Pesce (1567) gives the market a touch of style; built for the fishmongers of the Mercato Vecchio in what is now Piazza della Repubblica, it was dismantled when that square was laid out, and rebuilt here in 1951.

MERCATO DI SANT'AMBROGIO

Piazza Sant'Ambrogio. Mon–Sat 7am–2pm. MAP P.94–95, POCKET MAP H5

Out of the orbit of most tourists, the Mercato di Sant'Ambrogio is a smaller, tattier but equally enjoyable version of the San Lorenzo food hall. The *tavola calda* is one of Florence's lunchtime bargains, and – as at San Lorenzo – the stalls bring their prices down in the last hour of trading.

SCUOLA DEL CUOIO

Via San Giuseppe 5r ☎ 055 244 533, ⓦ www .scuoladelcuoio.com. Mon–Sat 9.30am–6pm, Sun 10am–6pm. MAP P.94–95, POCKET MAP G6

This academy for leather-workers sells bags, jackets, belts and other accessories at prices that compare very favourably with the shops. You won't find any startlingly original designs here, but the quality is very high and the staff are both knowledgeable and helpful.

Gelaterie

VESTRI

Borgo degli Albizi 11r ☎ 055 234 0374, ⓦ vestri.it. Mon–Sat 10am–8pm. MAP P.94–95, POCKET MAP F5

Chocoholics should make a bee-line for *Vestri*, where ice cream is just one of the concoctions on offer – there's also deliciously thick drinking chocolate and a mouth-watering array of sweets and other chocolate products. The ice cream comes in a dozen flavours, but the cocoa-based stuff is what they are renowned for.

VIVOLI

Via Isola delle Stinche 7r. Tues–Sun 7.30am–1am; closed Aug. MAP P.94–95, POCKET MAP F6

Operating from deceptively ordinary premises in a side street close to Santa Croce, this has long been rated the best ice-cream-maker in Florence – and some say in all of Italy.

SCUOLA DEL CUOIO

Cafés & bars

CAFFÈ CIBRÈO

Via Andrea del Verrocchio 5r ☎ 055 234 5853. Tues–Sat 8am–1am; closed 2 weeks in Aug. MAP P.94–95, POCKET MAP G5

Possibly the prettiest café in Florence, with a chi-chi clientele to match. Opened in 1989, the wood-panelled interior looks at least two hundred years older. Cakes and desserts are great, and the light meals bear the culinary stamp of the *Cibrèo* restaurant kitchens opposite (see opposite).

L'ANTICO NOÈ

Volta di San Piero 6r. Mon–Sat noon–3pm & 7pm–midnight. MAP P.94–95, POCKET MAP F5

The "Old Noah" is a long-established and utterly authentic stand-up wine bar, tucked into an uninviting little alley to the north of Santa Croce, at the end of Borgo Albizi. Excellent sandwiches and other snacks.

MOYO

Via de' Benci 23r ☎ 055 247 9738, ⓦ moyo .it. Mon–Thurs & Sun 8am–2am, Fri & Sat 9am–3am. MAP P.94–95, POCKET MAP F6

A young crowd flocks to this bar every evening – the food's pretty good (come for the early-evening *aperitivo* buffet) and the free wi-fi access is a plus, but it's the buzz that really brings them in. There's a DJ set on Monday, Wednesday and Thursday – everything from Latin to hip-hop.

REX CAFFÈ

Via Fiesolana 25r ☎ 055 248 0331. Mon & Wed–Sun 5pm–3am; closed June–Aug. MAP P.94–95, POCKET MAP G5

One of the city's real night-time fixtures, this is a friendly bar-club with a varied and loyal clientele. Vast curving lights droop over the central bar, which is studded with turquoise stone and broken mirror mosaics. Big arched spaces to either side mean there's plenty of room, the cocktails are good and the snacks excellent. DJs provide the sounds at weekends.

Restaurants

BALDOVINO

Via San Giuseppe 22r ☎ 055 241 773, ⓦ baldovino.com. Daily 11.30am–3.30pm & 7–11pm. MAP P.94–95, POCKET MAP G6

This superb place, established in the mid-1990s by Scottish expat David Gardner and his wife, is renowned for its pizzas (made in a wood-fired oven), but the main menu, which changes monthly, is full of good Tuscan and Italian dishes, with most mains at €12–17. Portions are very generous, and dining rooms – with boldly striped gold-and-brown walls – are a nice environment. The adjacent

REX CAFFÈ

BALDOVINO

café-bar – *Baldobar* – is good for a quick snack.

CIBRÈO

Via de' Macci 118r ☎ 055 234 1100, ⓦ edizioniteatrodelsalecibreofirenze.it. Tues–Sun 12.30–2.30pm & 7–11.15pm; closed Aug. MAP P.94–95, POCKET MAP G5

Fabio Picchi's *Cibrèo* is the first Florentine port-of-call for many foodies, having achieved fame well beyond the city. The recipe for success is simple: superb food with a creative take on Tuscan classics, served in a tastefully neo-traditional dining room by friendly and professional staff. You'll need to book days in advance for a table in the main part of the restaurant, but next door there's *Cibreino*, a small trattoria section where the food is of identical quality (though the menu is smaller), no bookings are taken and the prices are much lower: around €15 for the main course, as opposed to nearly €40 in the restaurant.

ENOTECA PINCHIORRI

Via Ghibellina 87 ☎ 055 242 777, ⓦ enotecapinchiorri.it. Tues 7.30–10pm, Thurs–Sat 12.30–2pm & 7.30–10pm; closed Aug. MAP P.94–95, POCKET MAP F6

This is the only Tuscan restaurant to have been given three Michelin stars, and no one seriously disputes *Pinchiorri*'s claim to be Florence's best restaurant. The food is as magnificent as the plaudits suggest, but the formality of the place is not to everyone's taste, and the prices are delirious: pasta dishes can cost as much as €70, main courses are €70–90, while the ever-changing set menus cost in the region of €250 per person, wine excluded – though you may get as many as twenty exquisite little dishes in the *menu degustazione*. The wine list has no equal in Italy, with some 150,000 bottles lying in the *Pinchiorri* cellars; bottles start at about €60, rising to five-figure sums.

IL FRANCESCANO

Largo Bargellini 16 ☎ 055 241 605, ⓦ ilfrancescano.com. Daily noon–2.30pm & 7–11pm. MAP P.94–95, POCKET MAP G6

Francescano began life as a sibling of neighbouring *Baldovino* (see opposite), and though it is now independently owned, it has a similar ambience, offering good food at fair prices (most mains are under €15), in an easy going, contemporary-trad setting. The lunchtime fixed menu is a bargain, and be sure to try one of the home-made desserts.

IL PIZZAIUOLO

Via de' Macci 113r ☎ 055 241 171, ⓦ ilpizzaiuolo.it. Mon–Sat 12.30–2.30pm & 7.30pm–midnight; closed Aug. MAP P.94–95, POCKET MAP G5

The Neapolitan pizzas here are among the best in the city (there are thirty varieties on offer), and the rest of the menu has a Neapolitan touch too – as does the atmosphere, which is friendly and high-spirited. The wine list, as you might expect, is full of southern Italian vintages rather than the usual Tuscans. Booking's a good idea, especially in the evening.

L'ANTICO NOÈ

Volta di San Piero 6r ☎ 055 234 0838,
🌐 lanticonoe.com. Mon–Sat noon–3pm &
7–11pm. MAP P.94–95, POCKET MAP F5

Situated next door to the
excellent *vinaio* of the same
name (see p.101), this tiny and
long-established trattoria is one
for hard-core carnivores – plate-
filling slabs of prime-quality
grilled meat are the only *secondi*
on offer. The decor is plain (you
sit on wicker-seated stools) but
the prices are not – expect to
pay around €25 for your steak.

LA PENTOLA DELL'ORO

Via di Mezzo 24r ☎ 055 241 808,
🌐 lapentoladelloro.it. Mon–Sat noon–3.30pm
& 9pm–midnight. MAP P.94–95, POCKET MAP G5

La Pentola has one of the more
imaginative menus in Florence,
mingling the innovative with
the profoundly traditional.
Some of the recipes used by
head chef Giuseppe Alessi date
back as far as the fourteenth
century, and there's a terrific
"Renaissance" set menu – a
bargain at €50 per person, wine
included. Most main courses
are less than €15, which is more
than reasonable for cooking of
this quality, even if the
basement dining room isn't the
most comfortable in the city.

OSTERIA DE' BENCI

OSTERIA CAFFÈ ITALIANO

Via Isola delle Stinche 11–13r ☎ 055 289 020,
🌐 osteriacaffeitaliano.com. Restaurant Tues–
Sun 12.30–2.30pm & 7.30–10.30pm; bar daily
10am–midnight. MAP P.94–95, POCKET MAP F6

The vaulted and cabinet-lined
main room of this upmarket
café-wine bar-restaurant is one
of the best-looking in Florence,
and the food more than lives
up to the setting. The cuisine is
typically Tuscan – lots of beef,
veal and wild boar – and
first-rate; expect to pay around
€20 for your main course.

OSTERIA DE' BENCI

Via de' Benci 13r ☎ 055 234 4923,
🌐 osteriadeibenci.it. Daily 12.15–3pm &
7.30–11pm. MAP P.94–95, POCKET MAP F6

The dining room of this modern
and popular *osteria* is
augmented by outside tables in
summer, and the moderately
priced menu (mains around
€15) consists of well-prepared
standards plus innovative takes
on Tuscan classics. Staff are
young and friendly, and the
atmosphere busy and informal.

SUD

Via della Vigna Vecchia 4r ☎ 055 289 368,
🌐 osteriacaffeitaliano.com. Tues–Sun
12.30–2.30pm & 7.30–10.30pm. MAP P.94–95,
POCKET MAP F6

This bright and smart bistro is
an offshoot of the *Osteria Caffè*

OSTERIA CAFFÈ ITALIANO

Italiano (see above), whose kitchen it shares. The menu draws on the cuisine of southern Italy, as the name implies, and is short but well-composed, with an emphasis on lightness – though there are a few pizzas on offer, this is not the place to come if you're ravenous. The *Tagliere misto* – slices of salami, cheese and vegetables (€12) makes an excellent lunch.

TEATRO DEL SALE

Via dei Macci 111r ☎ 055 200 1492, ⓦ edizioniteatrodelsalecibreofirenze.it. Tues-Sat 9am-3pm & 6pm-midnight. MAP P.94-95, POCKET MAP G5

Run by Fabio Picchi, the boss of *Cibrèo* (see p.101), this unique place is a combination of restaurant and cultural centre. You pay €7 annual membership (valid for one guest too), and then an extra amount to help yourself to the amazing buffets: €7 for breakfast (9–11am), €20 for lunch (noon–2.15pm), and €30 for dinner (7–9pm), when Picchi himself is often on duty in the open kitchen, announcing the dishes as they're put out. At 9.45pm guests are treated to a show, which might be anything from stand-up comedy to a piano recital or a dance group. If you don't want to eat, you can just hang out, drink coffee and browse through the books and magazines that are lying around. Needless to say, it's very popular, and reservations are advisable in the evenings.

Clubs & live music

JAZZ CLUB

Via Nuova de' Caccini 3 ☎ 055 247 9700. Tues-Fri 9pm-2am, Sat 9pm-3am; closed July & Aug. MAP P.94-95, POCKET MAP G4

Florence's foremost jazz venue. The €8 "membership" fee gets you down into the medieval brick-vaulted basement, where the atmosphere's informal and there's live music nearly every night (and an open jam-session on Tuesdays). Cocktails are good (if expensive), and you can also snack on bar nibbles, *focaccia* and desserts.

Y.A.G. B@R

Via de' Macci 8r ☎ 055 246 9022, ⓦ yagbar .com. Daily 8pm-3am. MAP P.94-95, POCKET MAP G6

The playlists may not be cutting-edge, but this large gay/ lesbian bar-club has been top of the pile for a long time simply because it's one of the friendliest places in town. No cover charge.

Theatre & classical music

TEATRO DELLA PERGOLA

Via della Pergola 18 ☎ 055 226 4316, ⓦ fondazioneteatrodellapergola.it. MAP P.94-95, POCKET MAP F5

The beautiful little Pergola was built in 1656 and is Italy's oldest surviving theatre. It plays host to top-flight instrumental recitals, chamber concerts and some of the best-known Italian theatre companies. The theatre season runs from October to April, and during the Maggio Musicale the Pergola is often used for small-scale operas.

TEATRO VERDI

Via Ghibellina 99–101 ☎ 055 212 320, ⓦ teatro verdionline.it. MAP P.94-95, POCKET MAP F6

One of the city's premier venues for classical music, musicals and mainstream theatre productions.

Oltrarno

The artisanal quarter of the city, the Oltrarno – literally "beyond the Arno" – contains several of the city's key sights. The biggest of these, Palazzo Pitti, is a colossal palace whose cluster of museums includes the city's second-ranking picture gallery, and whose garden, the Giardino di Bóboli, is Italy's most visited. Close by, the main church of Oltrarno, Santo Spirito, overlooks a piazza that typifies the gentrification that's happening in some parts of this quarter. From Santo Spirito it's a brief stroll to Santa Maria del Carmine, where the Cappella Brancacci contains an epoch-defining fresco cycle. On the other side of Oltrarno, the medieval Via dei Bardi and its continuation, Via San Niccolò, take you past the engagingly eclectic Museo Bardini, which you can visit en route to the Romanesque gem of San Miniato al Monte. Other major sights include Santa Felicita and the extraordinary waxworks of La Specola. And on top of all this, there's a greater concentration of good bars and restaurants here than in any other part of Florence – indeed, so popular has the Piazza Santo Spirito area become with tourists that it's known to some locals as "Santo Spiritoland", just as the equivalent on the other side of the river has been dubbed "Santa Croceland".

THE PONTE VECCHIO

MAP P.106–107, POCKET MAP B13

The direct route from the city centre to the heart of the Oltrarno crosses the Arno via the Ponte Vecchio, the "old bridge". Until 1218 the crossing here was the city's only bridge,

THE PONTE VECCHIO AT SUNRISE

SANTA FELICITA

though the version you see today dates from 1345, built to replace a wooden bridge swept away by floods twelve years earlier. The Ponte Vecchio has always been loaded with shops like those now propped over the water. Their earliest tenants were butchers and fishmongers, attracted to the site by the proximity of the river, which provided a convenient dumping ground for their waste. The current plethora of jewellers dates from 1593, when Ferdinando I evicted the butchers' stalls and other practitioners of what he called "vile arts". In their place he installed eight jewellers and 41 goldsmiths, also taking the opportunity to double the rents. Florence had long revered the art of the goldsmith, and several of its major artists were skilled in the craft: Ghiberti, Donatello and Cellini, for example. The third of this trio is celebrated by a bust in the centre of the bridge.

SANTA FELÌCITA

Piazza Santa Felicita. Mon–Sat 9.30am–12.30pm & 3.30–5.30pm. Free. MAP P.106–107, POCKET MAP D7

Some claim that Santa Felicita has an even longer lineage than San Lorenzo (see p.74), and that a church was founded here in the second century by Greek or Syrian merchants. What's known for certain is that a church existed on this site by the fifth century, by which time it had been dedicated to St Felicity; new churches were built in the eleventh and fourteenth centuries, then in 1565 Vasari added an elaborate portico to accommodate the *corridoio* linking the Uffizi and Palazzo Pitti; a window from the corridor looks directly into the church.

The interior demands a visit for the amazing Pontormo paintings in the **Cappella Capponi**, which lies to the right of the main door, surrounded by obstructive railings. The chapel was designed in the 1420s by Brunelleschi, but subsequently much altered – notably by Vasari, who destroyed the Pontormo fresco in the cupola when building his corridor. Under the cupola are four tondi of the Evangelists (painted with help from Pontormo's adoptive son, Bronzino), while on opposite sides of the window on the right wall are the Virgin and the angel of Pontormo's delightfully simple *Annunciation*. The low level of light admitted by this window was a determining factor in the startling colour scheme of the painter's *Deposition* (1525–28), one of the masterworks of Florentine Mannerism. Nothing in this picture is conventional: Mary is on a different scale from her attendants; the figures bearing Christ's body are androgynous beings clad in acidic sky-blue, puce green and candy-floss pink drapery; and there's no sign of the Cross, the thieves, or any of the other scene-setting devices usual in paintings of this subject.

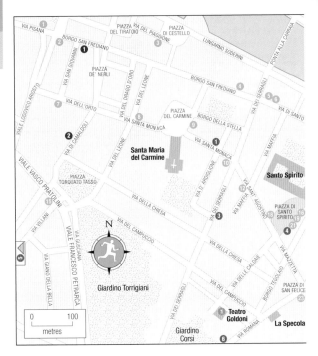

PALAZZO PITTI

Piazza Pitti ✪ uffizi.firenze.it. Galleria Palatina, Galleria d'Arte Moderna & Appartamenti Reali Tues–Sun 8.15am–6.50pm. €8.50, or €13 when special exhibitions are on. Museo degli Argenti, Galleria del Costume, Museo delle Porcellane & Giardino di Bóboli daily at 8.15am: Jan, Feb, Nov & Dec close 4.30pm; March close 5.30pm; April, May, Sept & Oct close 6.30pm; June–Aug close 7.30pm; closed 1st & last Mon of month. €10 joint ticket with Giardino Bardini. MAP P.106–107, POCKET MAP C7–D7

Beyond Santa Felìcita, the street opens out at Piazza Pitti, forecourt of the largest palace in Florence, the Palazzo Pitti. Banker and merchant Luca Pitti commissioned the palace in the 1450s to outdo his rivals, the Medici, but in 1549 the cash-strapped Pitti were forced to sell out – to the Medici. This subsequently became the Medicis' base in Florence, growing in bulk until the

seventeenth century, when it achieved its present gargantuan dimensions. Later, during Florence's brief tenure as the Italian capital between 1865 and 1871, it housed the Italian kings.

Today the Palazzo Pitti and the pavilions of the Giardino di Bóboli contain eight museums, of which the foremost is the **Galleria Palatina**, an art collection second in importance only to the Uffizi. The Palatina possesses superb works by Fra' Bartolomeo, Filippo and Filippino Lippi, Caravaggio, Rosso Fiorentino and Canova, no fewer than seventeen pieces by Andrea del Sarto, and numerous paintings by **Raphael** and **Titian**.

When Raphael settled in Florence in 1505, he was besieged with commissions from patrons delighted to find an artist for whom the creative

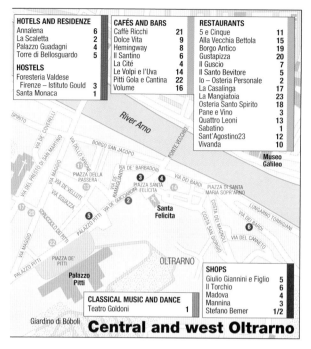

HOTELS AND RESIDENZE	
Annalena	6
La Scaletta	2
Palazzo Guadagni	4
Torre di Bellosguardo	5

HOSTELS	
Foresteria Valdese	
Firenze – Istituto Gould	3
Santa Monaca	1

CAFÉS AND BARS	
Caffè Ricchi	21
Dolce Vita	9
Hemingway	8
Il Santino	6
La Cité	4
Le Volpi e l'Uva	14
Pitti Gola e Cantina	22
Volume	16

RESTAURANTS	
5 e Cinque	11
Alla Vecchia Bettola	15
Borgo Antico	19
Gustapizza	20
Il Guscio	7
Il Santo Bevitore	5
Io – Osteria Personale	2
La Casalinga	17
La Mangiatoia	23
Osteria Santo Spirito	18
Pane e Vino	3
Quattro Leoni	13
Sabatino	1
Sant'Agostino23	12
Vivanda	10

CLASSICAL MUSIC AND DANCE	
Teatro Goldoni	1

SHOPS	
Giulio Giannini e Figlio	5
Il Torchio	6
Madova	4
Mannina	3
Stefano Bemer	1/2

Central and west Oltrarno

process involved so little agonizing. Among the masterpieces on show here are Raphael's portraits of Angelo Doni and his wife, Maddalena, and the wonderful *Madonna della Seggiola* (Madonna of the Chair), which was once Italy's most popular image of the Madonna – nineteenth-century copyists had to join a five-year waiting list to study the picture. According to Vasari, the model for the famous *Donna Velata* (Veiled Woman), in the Sala di Giove, was the painter's mistress, a Roman baker's daughter known to posterity as La Fornarina.

The paintings by Titian include a number of his most trenchant portraits. The lecherous and scurrilous Pietro Aretino – journalist, critic, poet and one of Titian's closest friends – was so thrilled by his portrait that he gave it to Cosimo I. Also here are likenesses of Philip II of Spain and the young Cardinal Ippolito de' Medici, also the so-called *Portrait of an Englishman*, who scrutinizes the viewer with unflinching sea-grey eyes. To his left, by way of contrast, is the same artist's sensuous and much-copied *Mary Magdalene*, the first of a series on this theme produced for the Duke of Urbino.

Much of the rest of the Pitti's first floor comprises the **Appartamenti Reali**, the Pitti's state rooms; after Raphael and Titian it can be difficult to sustain a great deal of enthusiasm for such ducal elegance, notwithstanding the sumptuousness of the furnishings.

On the floor above the Palatina is the **Galleria d'Arte Moderna**,

OLTRARNO

VIA DEL CANNETO

LUNGARNO TORRIGIANI

COSTA SCARPUCCIA

VIA DEI BARDI

PIAZZA DE' MOZZI

VIA DEI RENAI

PIAZZA NICOLA DEMIDOFF

Museo Stefano Bardini

VIA DI SAN NICCOLÒ

COSTA SAN GIORGIO

Giardino Bardini

Villa Bardini

Forte di Belvedere

VIA DI BELVEDERE

VIA DI BELVEDERE

VIALE GALILEO

VIA DE SAN LEONARDO

N

VIALE GALILEO

East Oltrarno

which comprises a chronological survey of primarily Tuscan art from the mid-eighteenth century to 1945. Much space is devoted to the work of the Macchiaioli (the open-air painters who were in some respects the Italian equivalent of the Impressionists), but there's a lot of mediocre stuff

THE PALAZZO PITTI

here, with ranks of academically proficient portraits, bombastic history paintings and sentimental dross such as Rodolfo Morgari's *Raphael Dying* and Gabriele Castagnola's depiction of Fra' Filippo Lippi on the brink of kissing the lovely young novice, Lucrezia Buti.

The **Museo degli Argenti**, entered from the main palace courtyard, is a colossal museum not just of silverware but of luxury artefacts in general. The craftsmanship on show is astounding, even if the final products are likely to strike you as being in dubious taste – room after room is packed with seashell figurines, cups made from ostrich eggs, portraits in stone inlay, bizarre ivory carvings, and the like. Amid all the trinkets, look out for the death mask of Lorenzo il Magnifico.

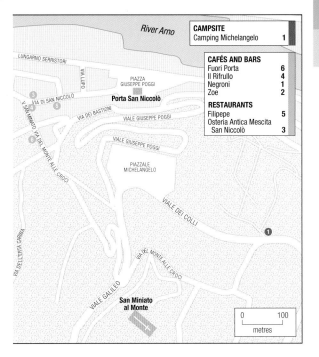

Visitors without a specialist interest are unlikely to be riveted by the two remaining museums currently open. In the Palazzina della Meridiana, the eighteenth-century southern wing of the Pitti, the **Galleria del Costume** provides the opportunity to see the dress that Eleonora di Toledo was buried in (it's the one she's wearing in Bronzino's portrait of her in the Palazzo Vecchio). The well-presented but esoteric collection of porcelain, the **Museo delle Porcellane**, is located at the top of the Bóboli Garden.

GIARDINO DI BÒBOLI

THE GIARDINO DI BÓBOLI

Opens daily at 8.15am; March closes 5.30pm; April, May, Sept & Oct closes 6.30pm; June–Aug closes 7.30pm; Nov–Feb closes 4.30pm; closed 1st & last Mon of month. €10 joint ticket with Museo degli Argenti, Museo delle Porcellane, Galleria del Costume & Giardino Bardini. MAP P.106–107, POCKET MAP B9–D7

GROTTA DEL BUONTALENTI

The land occupied by the formal gardens of the Palazzo Pitti, the Giardino di Bóboli, was once a quarry; the bedrock here is one of the sources of the yellow sandstone known as *pietra forte* (strong stone) that gives much of Florence its dominant hue. When the Medici acquired the house they set about transforming their back yard into an enormous garden, its every statue, view and grotto designed to elevate nature by the judicious application of art. The resulting landscape takes its name from the **Bóboli family**, erstwhile owners of some of the land. Opened to the public in 1766, this is the only really extensive area of accessible greenery in the centre of the city. It attracts some five million visitors annually, more than any other Italian garden.

Of all the garden's Mannerist embellishments, the most celebrated is the **Grotta del Buontalenti** (1583–88), to the left of the entrance, beyond Giambologna's much-repro-duced statue of Cosimo I's favourite dwarf astride a giant tortoise. Embedded in the grotto's faked stalactites and encrustations are replicas of Michelangelo's *Slaves* – the originals were lodged here until 1908. Lurking in the deepest recesses of the cave, and normally viewable only from afar, is Giambologna's *Venus Emerging from her Bath*, leered at by attendant imps.

Another spectacular set-piece is the fountain island called the **Isolotto**, which is the focal point of the far end of the garden; from within the Bóboli the most dramatic approach is along the central cypress avenue known as the **Viottolone**, many of whose statues are Roman originals.

The Forte di Belvedere

The Forte di Belvedere, standing on the crest of the hill above the Bóboli garden, was built by Buontalenti on the orders of Ferdinando I between 1590 and 1595, ostensibly to protect the city, but in fact to intimidate the grand duke's subjects. The panorama from here is superb, and exhibitions have often been held in and around the shed-like palace in the centre of the fortress, but in recent years two people died in falls from the fortress walls, and the city authorities have closed the place until further notice.

LA SPECOLA

Via Romana 17 ⓦ msn.unifi.it. Tues–Sun
9.30am–4.30pm. €6. MAP P.106–107,
POCKET MAP C8

On the third floor of the
university buildings on Via
Romana there lurks what can
reasonably claim to be the
strangest museum in the city.
Taking its name from the
telescope (*specola*) on its roof,
La Specola is a twin-sectioned
museum of zoology. The first
part is conventional enough,
with ranks of shells, insects and
crustaceans, followed by a
mortician's ark of animals
stuffed, pickled and desiccated.
Beyond some rather frayed-
looking sharks lie the things
everyone comes to see, the
Cere Anatomiche (Anatomical
Waxworks). Wax arms, legs and
organs cover the walls, arrayed
around satin beds on which
wax cadavers recline in
progressive stages of decon-
struction, each muscle fibre
and nerve cluster moulded and
dyed with absolute precision.
Most of the six hundred models
were made between 1775 and
1791 by Clemente Susini, and
were intended as teaching aids,
in an age when medical ethics
and refrigeration techniques
were not what they are today.

In a separate room towards
the end you'll find the grisliest
section of La Specola, a trio of
tableaux that were moulded in
the late seventeenth century
by **Gaetano Zumbo**, a cleric
from Sicily who was one of
the pioneers of the art of
anatomical waxwork. Whereas
Susini's masterpieces were
created to educate, these were
made to horrify, and to
horrify one man in particular:
the hypochondriacal Cosimo
III. Enclosed in tasteful
display cabinets, they depict
Florence during the plague,
with rats teasing the intestines
from rotting corpses, and the
pink bodies of the freshly
dead heaped on the suppu-
rating semi-decomposed. A
fourth tableau, illustrating the
horrors of syphilis, was
damaged in the 1966 flood,
and now consists of a loose
gathering of the deceased and
diseased. In the centre of the
room is displayed a dissected
waxwork head, built on the
foundation of a real skull; it's
as fastidious as any of Susini's
creations, but Zumbo couldn't
resist giving the skin a tint of
putrefaction, before applying a
dribble of blood to the mouth
and nose.

WAX CADAVER IN LA SPECOLA

SANTO SPIRITO

Piazza Santa Spirito. Mon, Tues & Thurs–Sat 9.30am–12.30pm & 4–5.30pm, Sun 4–5.30pm. Free. MAP P.106–107, POCKET MAP C7

Designed in 1434 as a replacement for a thirteenth-century church, Santo Spirito was one of Brunelleschi's last projects, a swansong later described by Bernini as "the most beautiful church in the world". Its plan is extremely sophisticated: a Latin cross with a continuous chain of 38 chapels round the outside and a line of 35 columns running without a break round the nave, transepts and chancel. The exterior wall was designed to follow the curves of the chapels' walls; as built, however, the exterior is plain and straight, and the facade was never completed. Inside, only the Baroque baldachin disrupts the harmony of Brunelleschi's design.

A fire in 1471 destroyed most of Santo Spirito's medieval works, including frescoes by Cimabue and the Gaddi family, but as a result the altar paintings comprise an unusually unified collection of religious works, the majority having been commissioned in the aftermath of the fire. Most prolific among the artists is the so-called **Maestro di Santo Spirito**, but the finest single painting is Filippino Lippi's *Nerli Altarpiece* (c. 1488), an age-darkened Madonna and Child with saints, which hangs in the south transept. A door in the north aisle leads through to Giuliano da Sangallo's stunning vestibule and **sacristy** (1489–93), the latter designed in imitation of Brunelleschi's Cappella dei Pazzi. Hanging above the altar is a delicate wooden crucifix attributed to the young Michelangelo.

The 1471 fire destroyed much of the rest of the monastery, with the exception of its refectory (entered to the left of the main church), which is now the home of the **Cenacolo di Santo Spirito** (Sat: April–Oct 9am–5pm; Nov–March 10.30am–1.30pm; €2.20), a one-room collection comprising an assortment of carvings, many of them Romanesque, and a huge fresco of *The Crucifixion* (1365) by Orcagna and his workshop.

SANTA MARIA DEL CARMINE

Piazza del Carmine ⓦ museicivici
fiorentini.it. Cappella Brancacci Mon &
Wed-Sat 10am–5pm, Sun 1–5pm. €6. Tickets
must be reserved at least one day in advance
on ☎ 055 276 8224 (daily 9am–5pm).
MAP P.106–107, POCKET MAP B6

In 1771 **fire** wrecked the
Carmelite convent and church
of Santa Maria del Carmine
some 300m west of Santo
Spirito, but somehow the
flames did not damage the
frescoes of the church's
Cappella Brancacci, a cycle of
paintings that is one of the
essential sights of Florence. The
chapel is barricaded off from
the rest of the Carmine, and
visits are restricted to a
maximum of thirty people at a
time, for an inadequate fifteen
minutes.

The decoration of the chapel
was begun in 1424 by
Masolino and **Masaccio**, when
the former was aged 41 and the
latter just 22. Within a short
time the elder was taking
lessons from the younger,
whose grasp of the texture of
the real world, of the principles
of perspective, and of the
dramatic potential of the

biblical texts they were
illustrating far exceeded that of
his precursors. In 1428
Masolino was called away to
Rome, where he was followed
by Masaccio a few months later.
Neither would return to the
chapel. Masaccio died the same
year, aged just 27, but, in the
words of Vasari, "All the most
celebrated sculptors and
painters since Masaccio's day
have become excellent and
illustrious by studying their art
in this chapel."

The Brancacci frescoes are as
startling as the Sistine Chapel
in Rome, the brightness and
delicacy of their colours and
the solidity of the figures
exemplifying what Bernard
Berenson singled out as the
tactile quality of Florentine art.
The small scene on the left of
the entrance arch is the
quintessence of Masaccio's art.
Depictions of **The Expulsion of
Adam and Eve** had never
before captured the desolation
of the sinners so graphically –
Adam presses his hands to his
face in bottomless despair, Eve
raises her head and screams. In
contrast, Masolino's dainty
Adam and Eve, opposite, pose
as if to have their portraits
painted.

St Peter is chief protagonist of
most of the remaining scenes,
some of which were left
unfinished in 1428 – work did
not resume until 1480, when
the frescoes were completed by
Filippino Lippi. One of the
scenes finished by Lippi is the
*Raising of Theophilus's Son and
St Peter Enthroned*, which
depicts St Peter bringing the
son of the Prefect of Antioch to
life and then preaching to the
people of the city. The three
figures to the right of his
throne are thought to be
Masaccio, Alberti and
Brunelleschi.

THE CAPPELLA BRANCACCI, SANTA MARIA DEL CARMINE

THE MUSEO STEFANO BARDINI

Piazza de' Mozzi 1 Ⓦ www.museicivicifiorentini
.it. Fri–Mon 11am–5pm. €6. MAP P.108–109.
POCKET MAP E7

The Museo Stefano Bardini, which stands at the end of the handsome Via de' Bardi, houses the collection of **Stefano Bardini** (1836–1922), once the most important art dealer in Italy, whose tireless activity laid the cornerstone of many important European and American museums. Determined that no visitor to his native city should remain unaware of his success, he bought the former monastery of San Gregorio alla Pace, and converted it into a vast house for himself and his collection. Sculpture, paintings, ceramics, armour, furniture, picture frames, carpets, wooden ceilings, tombstones – Bardini bought it all, and he bequeathed the whole lot to the city. Reopened in 2011 after a protracted restoration, the museum now looks much as it did when Bardini died, though a few pieces – notably Pietro Tacca's bronze boar and Giambologna's so-called *Diavolino* (Little Devil) – were added after his death.

The Bardini is more like a colossal **showroom** than a modern museum, with miscellaneous unlabelled objets d'art strewn all about the place, often following their owner's personal logic. The most interesting items are **upstairs**, where you'll find two reliefs of the *Madonna and Child* that may be by Donatello (in a room that's stacked with similar reliefs), a beautiful terracotta *Virgin Annunciate* from fifteenth-century Siena, and some fine drawings by Giambattista Tiepolo and his son Lorenzo. Most of the paintings are unremarkable, but there are exceptions, notably Guercino's *Atlas*, Michele Giambono's *St John the Evangelist*, and a *St Michael* by Antonio del Pollaiuolo. The main staircase is hung with gorgeous carpets, the largest of which was damaged by Hitler's spurs when it was laid out to welcome the Führer at Santa Maria Novella station.

GIARDINO BARDINI

Entrances at Costa di San Giorgio 2 and Via
de' Bardi 1r Ⓦ bardinipeyron.it. Opens daily at
8.15am; March closes 5.30pm; April, May,
Sept & Oct closes 6.30pm; June–Aug closes
7.30pm; Nov–Feb closes 4.30pm; closed 1st &
last Mon of month. €10 joint ticket with
Museo degli Argenti, Museo delle Porcellane,
Galleria del Costume & Giardino di Bóboli.
MAP P.108–109, POCKET MAP E8

The Giardino Bardini occupies the slope that was formerly the olive grove of the **Palazzo dei Mozzi**, a colossal house built in the late thirteenth century by the Mozzi family, at that time one of the richest families in Florence. (The palazzo houses a collection of seven hundred paintings donated to the city in 1937 by Fortunata Carobbi Corsi; there's a plan to put them on public show.)

GIARDINO BARDINI

After Stefano Bardini bought the property in 1913 he set about creating a semi-formal garden which has now been restored to the appearance he gave it, with a neo-Baroque staircase and terraces dividing the fruit-growing section from the miniature woodland of the "*bosco inglese*". At the summit of the garden, reached by a lovely long pergola of wisteria and hortensia, a colonnaded belvedere gives a splendid view of the city.

VILLA BARDINI

Costa di San Giorgio 2 ✆ bardinipeyron.it. Tues–Sun 10am–7pm. €8. MAP P.108–109, POCKET MAP E8

At the top of the Giardino Bardini stands the Villa Bardini, built in the seventeenth century and extended by Stefano Bardini. Having been thoroughly restored, the villa is used as an exhibition space and also houses a museum dedicated to **Pietro Annigoni** (1910–88), a vehemently anti-Modernist painter who was best known for his portraits of luminaries such as Pope John XXIII and Queen Elizabeth II. Fashionistas may enjoy the villa's collection of clothes created by Roberto

Capucci (born 1930). Dubbed the "Givenchy of Rome" by his admirers, Capucci made his name with frocks that seemed intent on upstaging their wearer – one of his most celebrated creations was a nine-layered dress that became famous when worn by a model in Cadillac ads in the 1950s.

THE CITY GATES AND PIAZZALE MICHELANGELO

MAP P.108–109, POCKET MAP G8

In medieval times San Niccolò was close to the edge of the city, and two of Florence's fourteenth-century gates still stand in the vicinity: the diminutive **Porta San Miniato**, set in a portion of the walls, and the huge **Porta San Niccolò**, overlooking the Arno. From either of these gates you can begin the climb up to San Miniato: the path from Porta San Niccolò weaves up through **Piazzale Michelangelo**, with its replica *David* and bumper-to-bumper tour coaches; the more direct path from Porta San Miniato offers a choice between the steep Via del Monte alle Croci or the stepped Via di San Salvatore al Monte, both of which emerge a short distance uphill from Piazzale Michelangelo.

SAN MINIATO AL MONTE

Via del Monte alle Croci. Daily: summer 8am–8pm; winter 8am–1pm & 3.30–7pm. Free. MAP P.108–109, POCKET MAP G9

Perhaps the finest Romanesque structure in Tuscany, San Miniato al Monte is also the oldest sacred building in Florence after the Baptistery. The dedicatee is **St Minias**, Florence's first home-grown martyr. Legend has it that after decapitation in the centre of the city the saintly corpse was seen to carry its severed head up the hill to this spot. A chapel devoted to Minias was built here in the eighth century, though construction of the present building began in 1013. Initially a Benedictine foundation, since 1373 it has belonged to the Olivetans, a Benedictine offshoot.

The lower part of the gorgeous marble facade is possibly eleventh-century, while the upper levels date from the twelfth century onwards, and were financed in part by the Arte di Calimala (cloth merchants' guild): their trademark, an eagle clutching a bale of cloth, perches up top.

The floor of the sublime **interior** is adorned by an elaborately patterned pavement that's dated 1207, while the middle of the nave is dominated by the lovely tabernacle designed in 1448 by Michelozzo. Steps either side of the tabernacle lead down to the **crypt**, where the original high altar contains the alleged bones of St Minias. Above, the **choir** and **presbytery** have a magnificent Romanesque pulpit and screen, and a great mosaic of *Christ Pantocrator*, created in 1297. Off the presbytery lies the **sacristy** (€1), whose walls are covered in a superlative fresco cycle by Spinello Aretino (1387), illustrating the life of St Benedict.

Back in the lower body of the church, off the left side of the nave, the **Cappella del Cardinale del Portogallo** constitutes one of Renaissance Florence's supreme examples of artistic collaboration. Completed in 1473, it was designed by Antonio di Manetto, a pupil and biographer of Brunelleschi, while the tomb was carved by Antonio and Bernardo Rossellino. The carefully integrated frescoes and paintings are by Alesso Baldovinetti, but Antonio and Piero del Pollaiuolo produced the main altarpiece (this is a copy, the original being in the Uffizi). The ceiling's tiled decoration and four glazed terracotta medallions were provided by Luca della Robbia.

Shops

GIULIO GIANNINI E FIGLIO

Piazza Pitti 36r ☎ 055 212 621, ⓦ www
.giuliogiannini.it. Mon–Sat 10am–7.30pm, Sun
10.30am–6.30pm. MAP P.106–107, POCKET MAP C7

Established in 1856, this
paper-making and book-
binding firm has been honoured
with exhibitions dedicated to its
work. Once the only place in
Florence to make its own
marbled papers, it now also
offers a wide variety of diaries,
address books and so forth.

IL TORCHIO

Via de' Bardi 17 ☎ 055 234 2862,
ⓦ legatoriailtorchio.com. Mon–Fri
9.30am–1.30pm & 2.30–7pm, Sat 9.30am–1pm.
MAP P.106–107, POCKET MAP E7

Founded in 1980 and now
owned by young Sicilian-
Canadian Erin Ciulla, Il Torchio
produces marbled paper, desk
accessories, diaries, albums and
other items in paper and leather.

MADOVA

Via Guicciardini 1r ☎ 055 239 6526,
ⓦ madova.com. Mon–Sat 10am–7pm.
MAP P.106–107, POCKET MAP D7

The last word in gloves – every
colour, every size, every style,
lined with lambswool, silk,
cashmere or nothing. Prices
range from around €40 to €200.

MANNINA

Via Guicciardini 16r ☎ 055 282 895,
ⓦ manninafirenze.com. Mon–Sat
9.30am–7.30pm, Sun 10.30am–1pm & 2–6pm.
MAP P.106–107, POCKET MAP D7

This famed Oltrarno
shoemaker has been going
since the 1950s, when it was
founded by Calogero Mannina,
father of the current boss,
Antonio. He produces
beautifully made and sensible
footwear at prices that are far
from extravagant – many styles
under €200 for women and
€400 for men.

STEFANO BEMER

Borgo San Frediano 143r ☎ 055 211 356,
ⓦ stefanobemer.it. Mon–Sat 9am–1pm &
3.30–7.30pm. MAP P.106–107, POCKET MAP A6

If you're in the market for
made-to-measure Italian shoes
of the very highest quality,
there's no better place than
this – prior to his premature
death in 2012, Stefano Bemer
was revered as perhaps Italy's
finest shoemaker, and his
apprentices continue to
produce footwear to Stefano's
demanding standards. Another
branch, close by at Via
Camaldoli 10r, is an outlet for
Bemer'S [sic], the off-the-peg
(but still expensive) footwear
designed by Stefano and his
brother Mario.

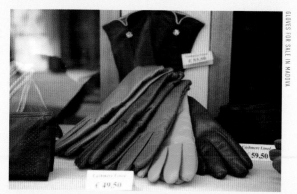

GLOVES FOR SALE IN MADOVA

Cafés & bars

FUORI PORTA

CAFFÈ RICCHI

Piazza di Santo Spirito 9r ☎ 055 215 864, ⓦ ricchiristorante.com. Summer Mon–Sat 7am–1am; winter closes 10pm; closed last 2 weeks of Feb & Aug. MAP P.106–107, POCKET MAP C7

In business since 1957, this is the oldest and the smartest of the café-bars on this square, with a good selection of cakes, ice cream and lunchtime snacks, and superb coffee. The owners of the *Ricchi* also have a good restaurant next door, and run the *Cabiria* bar at no. 4r on the piazza.

DOLCE VITA

Piazza del Carmine ☎ 055 284 595. ⓦ dolcevitaflorence.com. Daily 7pm–2am. MAP P.106–107, POCKET MAP B6

This smart and extremely popular bar with a buzzy outdoor terrace has been going for more than 25 years and has stayed ahead of the game by constantly updating. Install yourself on one of the bar stools and preen with Florence's beautiful young things. There's live music (Latin, rock or jazz) Tues from 7.30pm, a DJ other nights, and *aperitivi* every night 7.30–10pm.

FUORI PORTA

Via del Monte alle Croci 10r ☎ 055 234 2483. ⓦ fuoriporta.it. Daily: April–Sept 12.30pm–12.30am; Oct–March Mon–Fri 12.30–3.30pm & 7pm–12.30am, Sat & Sun 12.30pm–12.30am. MAP P.108–109, POCKET MAP F8

If you're climbing up to San Miniato you could take a breather at this justly famous wine bar-*osteria*. There are over five hundred wines to choose from by the bottle, and an ever-changing selection of wines by the glass, as well as a wide selection of grappas and malt whiskies. Bread, cheese, ham and salami are available,

together with a choice of pasta dishes and tasty *secondi*, mainly around €10.

HEMINGWAY

Piazza Piattellina 9r ☎ 055 284 781. Mon–Thurs & Sun 4.30pm–1am, Fri & Sat closes 2am; closed mid-June to mid-Sept. MAP P.106–107, POCKET MAP B6

Owners Paul de Bondt and Andrea Slitti are members of the Compagnia del Cioccolato, a chocolate appreciation society – and it shows: the chocolate desserts and handmade chocolates are sublime. You can also choose from one of countless speciality teas, sample over twenty coffees, or knock back one of the "tea cocktails".

IL RIFRULLO

Via San Niccolò 53–57r ☎ 055 234 2621, ⓦ ilrifrullo.com. Daily 8am–2am; closed 2 weeks in Aug. MAP P.108–109, POCKET MAP F8

Lying to the east of the Ponte Vecchio–Pitti Palace route, this place attracts fewer tourists than many Oltrarno café-bars. Delicious snacks with the early-evening *aperitivi* (when the music gets turned up), as well as more substantial (and quite pricey) dishes in the restaurant section. There's a pleasant garden terrace, too.

IL SANTINO

Via Santo Spirito 60r ☎ 055 230 2820. Daily 10.30am–11pm. MAP P.106–107, POCKET MAP C6

This small gastronomic

alimentari-cum-wine bar is an offshoot of the neighbouring *Santo Bevitore* (see p.121), and is proving just as successful. The wines on offer are top quality, as are the snacks.

LA CITÉ

Borgo San Frediano 20r ☎ 055 210 387, ⓦ lacitelibreria.info. Mon–Sat 10am–1am, Sun noon–1am. MAP P.106–107, POCKET MAP B6

With its huge windows, mezzanine balcony and shelves of books (to buy or just to browse), this café-bar-bookshop has an arty quasi-Parisian ambience. An area is set aside for live performances (usually music).

LE VOLPI E L'UVA

Piazza dei Rossi 1r ☎ 055 239 8132, ⓦ www .levolpieluva.com. Mon–Sat 11am–9pm. MAP P.106–107, POCKET MAP D7

This discreet, friendly little *enoteca* does good business by concentrating on the wines of small producers and providing tasty cold meats and snacks to accompany them (the selection of cheeses is tremendous). At any one time you can choose from at least two dozen different wines by the glass. In summer the shady terrace is a very pleasant refuge from the heat.

NEGRONI

Via dei Renai 17r ☎ 055 243 647, ⓦ negronibar.it. Mon–Fri 8pm–3am, Sat & Sun 7pm–3am; closed two weeks in Aug. MAP P.108–109, POCKET MAP F7

Set back from the Arno, on the south side of the grassy Piazza Demidoff, *Negroni* has been a fixture on the Florentine scene for years. It takes its name from the cocktail (gin+vermouth+ Campari) created on this spot for Count Camillo Negroni way back at the start of the last century, and cocktails are still a major attraction, along with the

VOLUME

early-evening *aperitivo* buffet and the music – there's a DJ most nights.

PITTI GOLA E CANTINA

Piazza Pitti 16 ☎ 055 212 704. ⓦ pittigolaecantina.com. Daily 1pm–midnight; closed 2 weeks in mid-Aug. MAP P.106–107, POCKET MAP C7

Small and friendly wine bar, run by knowledgeable people; the food – mainly cold meats and handmade pasta – is good.

VOLUME

Piazza Santo Spirito 5r ☎ 055 2381 460, ⓦ volumefirenze.com. Mon & Wed–Sun 11.30am–1am. MAP P.106–107, POCKET MAP C7

This is the most idiosyncratic of the bar-cafés on Piazza Santo Spirito – it used to be a workshop used by makers of hat forms, and the walls of the front room are still hung with the tools of the trade. Art works and craft items are on display in the cosy back room, along with books (*Volume* markets itself as "il caffè culturale"), and there's often live music in the evening – otherwise, expect a DJ. The atmosphere is hip and relaxed, and it's invariably busy, as are its neighbours, *Cabiria* and *Popcafé*.

ZOE

Via dei Renai 13 ☎ 055 243 111, ⓦ zoebar.it. Mon–Thurs 8am–1.30am, Fri & Sat 8am–3am, Sun 6pm–1am. MAP P.108–109, POCKET MAP F7

Like the neighbouring *Negroni* (see p.119), *Zoe* is perennially popular for summer evening drinks, but also attracts lots of young Florentines right through the day. Breakfast is served from 8am–noon, lunch from noon–4pm, then it's "Aperitif" from 5–10pm (the Crimson Zoe cocktail is notorious) before the DJ gets the partying started. It also does good snacks and simple meals, and it's something of an art venue too.

Restaurants

5 E CINQUE

Piazza della Passera 1 ☎ 055 274 1585. Tues–Sun noon–10pm. MAP P.106–107, POCKET MAP C7

This busy little café-restaurant is one of the city's rare havens for vegetarians, as dishes made from organic vegetables are the focus – the wines are organic too. It's more a place for a quick and light meal than a lingering evening, but the food is good and the staff very warm. No credit cards.

ALLA VECCHIA BETTOLA

Viale Vasco Pratolini 3–7 ☎ 055 224 158, ⓦ www.florence.ala.it/bettola. Tues–Sat noon–2.30pm & 7.30–10.30pm. MAP P.106–107, POCKET MAP A7

Located on a major traffic intersection a couple of minutes' walk from the Carmine, this wonderfully old-fashioned place – with its marble-topped tables – has something of the atmosphere of an old-style drinking den, which is what it once was; it boasts a good repertoire of Tuscan meat dishes, with main courses mostly €12–15. No credit cards.

BORGO ANTICO

Piazza di Santo Spirito 6r ☎ 055 210 437, ⓦ borgoanticofirenze.com. Daily noon–midnight. MAP P.106–107, POCKET MAP C7

The spartan chic of *Borgo Antico*'s white-tile and pink-plaster decor reflects the increasingly trendy character of this once notoriously sleazy Oltrarno piazza. In summer the outside tables here are invariably packed, and the majority of the clientele are usually foreigners. But *Borgo Antico* is not one of Florence's cynical tourist-traps: the food (pizza plus Tuscan standards) is generally good, prices are fair, and the servings are generous to a fault.

FILIPEPE

Via San Niccolò 39r ☎ 055 200 1397, ⓦ filipepe.com. Daily 7.30pm–11pm; closed 2 weeks in Aug. MAP P.108–109, POCKET MAP F8

Filipepe has a menu that's markedly different from most of the competition – it markets itself as a "Mediterranean restaurant", and offers delicious food drawn from a variety of Italian regional cuisines. The wine list is similarly wide-ranging, and the decor offbeat and attractive. Most main courses are around the €20 range.

GUSTAPIZZA

Via Maggio 46r. Tues–Sun 11.30am–3pm & 7–11pm. MAP P.106–107, POCKET MAP C7

The wood-fired Neapolitan pizzas served here are the best in Oltrarno – and pizzas are all they do, which is always a good thing. It's cheap, busy and basic, and no reservations are taken, so be prepared to queue.

IL GUSCIO

Via dell'Orto 49 ☎ 055 224 421, ⓦ www .il-guscio.it. Mon–Fri noon–2pm & 8–11pm, Sat 8–11pm only; closed Aug. MAP P.106–107, POCKET MAP A6

This smart rustic-style restaurant is a long-estab-lished Oltrano favourite: high-quality Tuscan meat and fish dishes, superb desserts and a wide-ranging wine list.

And it's not terribly pricey – you'll pay in the region of €40 per person.

IL SANTO BEVITORE

Via Santo Spirito 64–66r ☎ 055 211 264, ⓦ ilsantobevitore.com. Mon–Sat 12.30–3pm & 7.30–11.30pm, Sun 7.30–11.30pm. MAP P.106–107, POCKET MAP C6

"The Holy Drinker" is an airy, stylish and hugely popular gastronomic *enoteca* with a small but classy menu of seasonal food (around €35 for a meal without drinks) to complement its enticing wine list. Very busy throughout the year, especially in the evenings, so you'd best book a table. The platters of cold meats and cheese make an excellent lunch.

IO – OSTERIA PERSONALE

Borgo San Frediano 167r ☎ 055 933 1341, ⓦ io-osteriapersonale.it. Mon–Sat 8–10.30pm. MAP P.106–107, POCKET MAP A6

Run by a young and imaginative team, this is one of the very best restaurants to have opened in Florence in recent years. The minimalist decor – bare brick walls and very upright chairs – send out the message that this place is serious about its food, and not just another purveyor of routine Tuscan recipes. There are no antipasti or pasta courses here, and no *bistecca* – what you get instead is an inventive and concise array of seafood and meat dishes (main courses around €20), with the option of selecting your own tasting menus at €40 or €55. Ingredients are seasonal and local (the suppliers are listed on the menu) and the wines come from small vineyards, as you might expect from a restaurant that is underpinned by personal values.

GUSTAPIZZA

LA CASALINGA

LA CASALINGA

Via del Michelozzo 9r ☎ 055 218 624,
ⓦ trattorialacasalinga.it. Mon–Sat
noon–2.30pm & 7–10pm; closed last 3 weeks
of Aug. MAP P.106–107, POCKET MAP C7

Located in a side street off
Piazza di Santo Spirito, this
long-established family-run
trattoria serves up some of the
best low-cost Tuscan dishes in
town. No frills – paper
tablecloths, so-so house wine
by the flask and brisk service –
but most nights it's filled with
regulars and some tourists, and
if you turn up after 8pm
without a reservation you'll
almost certainly have to queue.

LA MANGIATOIA

Piazza San Felice 8–9r ☎ 055 224 060.
Tues–Sun noon–3pm & 7–10pm. MAP P.106–107,
POCKET MAP C7

Ideally placed for lunch before
or after a visit to Palazzo Pitti,
this *rosticceria–pizzeria* has a
no-frills trattoria out back,
where a full menu of Tuscan
fare is served in a bright and
somewhat spartan interior,
with most *secondi* less than
€10. The pizzas, cooked in a
wood-fired oven, are good too.

OSTERIA ANTICA MESCITA SAN NICCOLÒ

Via San Niccolò 60r ☎ 055 234 2836,
ⓦ osteriasanniccolo.it. Mon–Sat 12.30–3pm

& 7pm–midnight; closed Aug. MAP P.108–109,
POCKET MAP F8

This genuine old-style *osteria*
has a small menu of robust and
well-prepared Florentine
staples (*ribollita*, *lampredotto*,
etc), at around €10–15 for main
courses. The downstairs dining
room is an atmospheric spot –
it was formerly a crypt of the
adjacent church of San Niccolò.

OSTERIA SANTO SPIRITO

Piazza di Santo Spirito 16r ☎ 055 238 2383,
ⓦ osteriasantospirito.it. Daily 12.30–2.30pm
& 8pm–midnight. MAP P.106–107, POCKET MAP C7

Run by the owners of the *Borgo
Antico* (see p.120), this modern
osteria is likewise a place that
aims to please the tourists yet
does so without sacrificing its
integrity. The menu is full of
the usual Tuscan meat and fish
dishes, but with a touch of
contemporary flair – and the
portions are substantial. Tables
are on two floors, and in
summer you can eat outdoors
on the piazza. Main courses
€15–25.

PANE E VINO

Piazza di Cestello 3r ☎ 055 247 6956,
ⓦ ristorantepaneevino.it. Mon–Sat 7.30pm–
midnight; closed 2 weeks in Aug. MAP P.106–107,
POCKET MAP B6

Pane e Vino began life as a wine
bar (in a different part of
Oltrarno), so it's no surprise
that the wine list is well
selected, with good Tuscans for
less than €20. The ambience is
stylish yet relaxed (the dining
room is like an elegant barn)
and the menu small and
consistently excellent (*secondi*
€15–20), featuring an enticing
five-course set menu at €45,
excluding drinks.

QUATTRO LEONI

Via dei Vellutini 1r/Piazza della Passera
☎ 055 218 562. ⓦ 4leoni.com. Daily noon–
midnight. MAP P.106–107, POCKET MAP C7

One of the most pleasant places to eat in Florence: inside, there are three rooms with splashy modern paintings hung on the rough stone walls; outside, the tables are shaded by vast canvas umbrellas in a corner of the tiny Piazza della Passera. Some say the quality of the food and service has declined slightly with its rising popularity, but it's never less than a cut above the average, and the youthful vibe is refreshing. Expect to pay around €15 for a main course.

SABATINO

Via Pisani 2r ☎ 055 225 955. Mon–Fri noon–2.30pm & 7.15pm–10pm; closed Aug. MAP P.106–107, POCKET MAP A5

The cooking at *Sabatino* is as plain as can be, as is the place itself – there's one refectory-like dining room, with big tables covered with laminated chequered cloth. But this old-fashioned family *osteria* is absolutely authentic, and it's ridiculously inexpensive.

SANT'AGOSTINO23

Via Sant'Agostino 23r ☎ 055 210 208, ⓦ santagostinofirenze.com. Tues–Sun 12.30–2.30pm & 7.30–10.45pm. MAP P.106–107, POCKET MAP B7

This newish trattoria is a touch less touristy than those on nearby Campo Santo Spirito, though the presence of (excellent) hamburgers on the otherwise traditional Tuscan menu does suggest that they have at least one eye on the Anglo-Americans. Main courses are around €15, and the pasta dishes are particularly good. And the dark decor of the four small dining rooms is interestingly unusual.

VIVANDA

Via Santa Monaca 7r ☎ 055 238 1208, ⓦ vivandafirenze.it. Daily 12.30–11.30pm. MAP P.106–107, POCKET MAP B6

Florence's first organic *enoteca* is also a small self-service restaurant, offering meals that use vegetables from *Vivanda*'s own farm. The vegetarian dishes are good, if quite pricey given the size of the portions, but there are set menus for as little as €20.

Classical music & dance

TEATRO GOLDONI

Via Santa Maria 15 ☎ 055 210 804. MAP P.106–107, POCKET MAP B8

This exquisite little theatre, inaugurated in 1817 and seating just 363 people, is used for chamber music, opera and dance performances.

QUATTRO LEONI

The city outskirts

Two of the attractions covered in this section – the Museo Stibbert and Florence's football ground – are a stiff walk from the centre of town, but can be reached by ATAF bus; the Cascine park is a stroll west from the Ognissanti district.

THE CASCINE

Bus #1, 9, 12, 17 or 17c from the station.
MAP P.125, POCKET MAP A3

Florence's **public park**, the Cascine, begins close to the Ponte della Vittoria, a half-hour walk west of the Ponte Vecchio, and dwindles away 3km downstream, at the confluence of the Arno and the Mugnone rivers. Once a dairy farm (*cascina*), then a hunting reserve, this narrow strip of greenery mutated into a high-society venue in the eighteenth century: Florence's *beau monde* used to relax with a promenade under the trees of the Cascine. A fountain in the park bears a dedication to Shelley, who was inspired to write his *Ode to the West Wind* while strolling here on a blustery day in 1819.

Thousands of people come out here on Tuesday mornings for the colossal **market**, and on any day of the week the Cascine swarms with joggers, cyclists and roller-bladers. Parents bring their kids out here too, but it has to be said that the Cascine is a somewhat ill-kempt park, and it also has a reputation as a haunt for the city's junkies. It's emphatically not a place for a nocturnal stroll, as it has long been a hunting ground for the city's pimps.

STROLLING THROUGH THE CASCINE

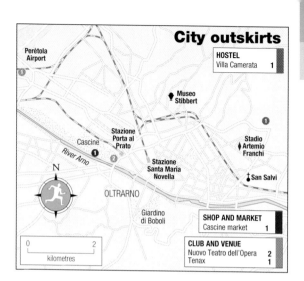

City outskirts

HOSTEL	
Villa Camerata	1

SHOP AND MARKET	
Cascine market	1

CLUB AND VENUE	
Nuovo Teatro dell'Opera	2
Tenax	1

THE MUSEO STIBBERT

Via Stibbert 26 ⓦ museostibbert.it. Mon–Wed 10am–2pm, Fri–Sun 10am–6pm. One-hour guided tour €6. Bus #4 from the station. MAP P.125, POCKET MAP E1

About 1500m north of San Marco stands the Museo Stibbert. This rambling, murky mansion was the home of the half-Scottish-half-Italian Frederick Stibbert, who in his twenties made a name for himself in Garibaldi's army. Later he inherited a fourteenth-century house from his mother, then bought the neighbouring mansion and joined the two together, thus creating a place big enough to accommodate the fruits of his compulsive collecting. The 64 rooms contain over fifty thousand items, ranging from snuffboxes to paintings by Carlo Crivelli and a possible Botticelli.

Militaria were Frederick's chief enthusiasm, and the Stibbert **armour** collection is reckoned one of the world's best. It includes Roman, Etruscan and Japanese examples (the highlight of the whole museum), as well as a fifteenth-century *condottiere*'s outfit and the armour worn by the great Medici soldier Giovanni delle Bande Nere, retrieved from his grave in San Lorenzo in 1857. The big production number comes in the great hall, between the two houses, where a platoon of mannequins is clad in full sixteenth-century gear.

THE MUSEO STIBBERT

STADIO ARTEMIO FRANCHI

Viale Manfredo Fanti ⓦ en.violachannel.tv. Bus #17 from the train station. MAP P.125, POCKET MAP H3

As befits this monument-stuffed city, Florence's football team play in a **stadium** that's listed as a building of cultural significance, the Stadio Artemio Franchi (or Stadio Comunale) at Campo di Marte. It was designed by Pier Luigi Nervi in 1930, and was the first major sports venue to exploit the shape-making potential of reinforced concrete – its spiral ramps, cantilevered roof and slim central tower still make quite an impact.

Following bankruptcy in 2002, Florence's football team – AC Fiorentina (ⓦ en.viola channel.tv) – was kicked out of Serie A and demoted to Serie C2B, the bottom of the heap. Most of its star players jumped ship, but the club fought its way back up the leagues, returning to Serie A for the 2004/2005 season. AC Fiorentina (known as The Viola, after their violet shirts) are now once again a securely top-flight outfit. Tickets cost from around €20 and can be bought at the ground itself or from numerous outlets in the city, the chief of which are Box Office (see p.7) and the kiosk in Via Anselmi, off Piazza della Repubblica; other points of sale are listed on the club website.

SAN SALVI

Via San Salvi 16. Tues–Sun 8.15am–1.50pm. Free. Bus #10 from the train station, or #6 from Piazza San Marco. MAP P.125, POCKET MAP H5

Twenty minutes' walk beyond Piazza Beccaria, east of Sant'Ambrogio, is the ex-convent of San Salvi, where the most precious possession is a glorious *Last Supper* by Andrea del Sarto. As a prelude to this picture, there's a gallery of fairly unremarkable Renaissance art, and some beautiful reliefs from the tomb of Giovanni Gualberto, founder of the Vallombrosan order to which this monastery belonged. The tomb was smashed up by Charles V's troops in 1530 but they refused to damage the *Last Supper*, which is still in the refectory for which it was painted, accompanied by a pair of del Sarto frescoes brought here from other churches in Florence.

STADIO ARTEMIO FRANCHI

Market

CASCINE MARKET

Tuesday mornings. MAP P.125, POCKET MAP A3

The biggest of all Florence's markets takes place on Tuesday mornings at the Cascine park, near the banks of the Arno, where hundreds of stallholders set up an alfresco budget-class department store. Clothes (some secondhand) and shoes are the best bargains.

Club & venue

NUOVO TEATRO DELL'OPERA

Viale Fratelli Rosselli 1 ☎ 055 277 9350, 🌐 maggiofiorentino.com. MAP P.125, POCKET MAP A3

The city's hi-tech new concert hall is the centrepiece of the "Parco della Musica", a cultural zone that's being developed on the edge of the Cascine park. For operas and other big events there's a 1800-seat auditorium,

complemented by a 1100-seater for recitals and a terrace for open-air performances. When we went to press, the complex was incomplete – the city and authorities hope that Rome will help them to raise the €46 million needed to finish the next stage.

TENAX

Via Pratese 46 ☎ 055 282 340. Thurs–Sat 10.30pm–4am; closed mid-May to mid-Sept. MAP P.125, POCKET MAP A3

Florence's top-ranking club, the warehouse-styled *Tenax* hosts big-name DJs. As it's located northwest, near the airport (take a taxi), you'll escape the *internazionalisti* who tend to pack the central clubs. With two large floors, it's a venue for concerts as well. In summer, when the club is shut, *Tenax* often holds one-off events at the Stazione Leopoldina, a disused train station by the new opera house. Admission from around €20.

Fashion factory outlets

Tuscany is the powerhouse of the country's textile industry, and several retail outlets within easy reach of Florence sell each season's leftovers at discounts as high as seventy percent.

Barberino Designer Outlet Via Meucci, Barberino di Mugello ☎ 055 842 161, 🌐 mcarthurglen.it/barberino. The biggest outlet, with more than 100 shops, including Cavalli, Missoni and Prada. SITA bus from Via Santa Caterina da Siena or shuttle bus from outside Santa Maria Novella station (2 daily). Tues–Fri 10am–8pm, Sat & Sun 10am–9pm.

Dolce & Gabbana Via Pian dell'Isola 49, Località Santa Maria Maddalena ☎ 055 833 1300. This two-storey shed is packed with clothes, accessories and household items from Dolce & Gabbana. Train to Rignano sull'Arno-Reggello, then a taxi. Daily 10am–7.30pm.

The Mall Via Europa 8, Leccio Regello ☎ 055 865 7775, 🌐 themall.it. Outlets for Cavalli, Pucci, Armani and Ferragamo, among others, but Gucci is the dominant presence. SITA bus from Via Santa Caterina da Siena or shuttle bus from outside Santa Maria Novella station (2 daily). Daily 10am–7pm.

Space Levanella Montevarchi ☎ 055 91 901. This outlet is stacked with Prada clothes, as well as a good selection from the Miu Miu diffusion label. Train to Montevarchi, then a taxi. Sun–Fri 10.30am–8pm, Sat 9.30am–8pm.

Fiesole

The hill-town of Fiesole, which spreads over a cluster of hills above the Mugnone and Arno valleys some 8km northeast of Florence, is conventionally described as a pleasant retreat from the crowds and heat of summertime Florence. Unfortunately, its tranquillity has been so well advertised that in high season it's now hardly less busy than Florence itself; that said, Fiesole offers a grandstand view of the city, has something of the feel of a country village, and bears many traces of its long history. First settled in the Bronze Age, later by the Etruscans and then absorbed by the Romans, it rivalled its neighbour until the early twelfth century, when the Florentines overran the town. From that time it became a satellite, favoured as a semi-rural second home for wealthier citizens such as the ubiquitous Medici.

The #7 ATAF bus runs every twenty minutes from Via La Pira (near the junction with Piazza San Marco) to Fiesole's central Piazza Mino da Fiesole; the journey takes around twenty minutes.

THE DUOMO

Mon–Sat 7.30am–noon, Sun 7.30am–1pm. Free. MAP P.129

When the Florentines wrecked Fiesole in 1125, the only major building they spared was the Duomo, on the edge of Piazza Mino. Subsequently, nineteenth-century restorers managed to ruin the exterior, which is now notable only for its lofty campanile. The most interesting part of the bare interior is the raised choir: the altarpiece is a polyptych, painted in the 1440s by Bicci di Lorenzo, and the Cappella Salutati, to the right, contains two fine pieces carved around the same time by Mino da Fiesole – an altar frontal of *The Madonna and Saints* and

PIAZZA MINO DA FIESOLE

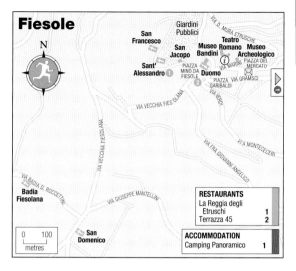

the tomb of Bishop Salutati.
Fiesole's patron saint,
St Romulus, is buried
underneath the choir in the
ancient crypt.

THE MUSEO BANDINI

Via Dupré 1 ☻ museidifiesole.it. Mon &
Wed–Sun from 10am: March & Oct closes
6pm; April–Sept closes 7pm; Nov–Feb
closes 2pm. €10 one-day ticket for all
Fiesole's museums (€8 Mon–Thurs).
MAP P.129

The Museo Bandini possesses
a workaday collection of
glazed terracotta in the
style of the della Robbias,
the odd piece of Byzantine
ivory work and a few
thirteenth- and fourteenth-
century Tuscan pictures,
none of them especially
outstanding.

TEATRO ROMANO AND MUSEO
ARCHEOLOGICO

Via Portigiani 1 ☻ museidifiesole.it.
Mon & Wed–Sun opens 10am: March & Oct
closes 6pm; April–Sept closes 7pm; Nov–Feb
closes 2pm. €10 ticket with Museo Bandini
(€8 Mon–Thurs). MAP P.129

Built in the first century BC,
the three-thousand-seat Teatro
Romano was excavated
towards the end of the
nineteenth century and is in
such good repair that it's used
for performances during the
Estate Fiesolana festival
(see p.149). Most of the
exhibits in the site's small
museum were excavated in
this area, and encompass
pieces from the Bronze Age
to the Roman occupation.

SAN JACOPO

Via San Francesco. Summer Sat & Sun
10am–7pm; winter closes 5pm. Free.
MAP P.129

From the piazza, the steep
Via San Francesco runs past
the **Oratorio di San Jacopo**, a
little chapel containing a
fifteenth-century fresco of *The
Coronation of the Virgin* and
some fine examples of
ecclesiastical goldsmithing. A
little further up, on the left, a
terrace in front of the town's
war memorials offers a
knockout **view** of Florence.

SANT'ALESSANDRO

Via San Francesco. Free. MAP P.129

The church of Sant'Alessandro, at the top of Via San Francesco, was founded in the sixth century on the site of Etruscan and Roman temples; repairs have rendered the outside a whitewashed nonentity, but the beautiful *marmorino cipollino* (onion marble) columns of the basilical interior make it the most atmospheric building in Fiesole. The bases and Ionic capitals of the columns were recycled from Roman structures. From time to time the church is used as an exhibition space; otherwise, it's very rarely open.

SAN FRANCESCO

Via San Francesco. Daily: April–Sept 9am–noon & 3–7pm; Oct–March 9am–noon & 3–6pm. Free. MAP P.129

The site of Fiesole's Etruscan acropolis is occupied by the fourteenth-century monastery of San Francesco. Its tranquil little church – which was rebuilt in neo-Gothic style in the first decade of the twentieth century – contains an *Immaculate Conception* by Piero di Cosimo (second altar on the right), and has a fine main altarpiece by Neri di Bicci. In the monastery's tiny **museum** (free) you can see a miscellany of mostly unlabelled material, much of it gathered in the course of missions to the Far East; alongside the Ming and Qing vases, there's a small array of stuff from ancient Egypt. To the right of the church is a tiny and bucolic cloister, which usually can be admired only through the gate. From the front of San Francesco a gate opens into the wooded Giardino Pubblico, the most pleasant descent back to Piazza Mino; on the way down,

you'll get a good view of the Roman ruins.

SAN DOMENICO

Piazza San Domenico. Summer 7.30am–12.30pm & 4.30–6.30pm; winter 8.30am–noon & 4–6pm. Free. MAP P.129

The most enjoyable excursion from Fiesole is a wander down the narrow Via Vecchia Fiesolana, which passes the **Villa Medici** – built for Cosimo il Vecchio by Michelozzo – on its way to the hamlet of San Domenico. Fra' Angelico entered the Dominican order at the monastery of San Domenico, and the church retains a *Madonna and Angels* by him – it was painted for the high altar but is now in the first chapel on the left. The adjacent chapterhouse also has a Fra' Angelico fresco of *The Crucifixion* and a *Madonna and Child* that's been attributed to him; for admission, ring at no. 4, to the right of the church. The bus back to Florence stops at San Domenico, so you don't have to trudge back up to Piazza Mino to catch it.

THE BADÌA FIESOLANA

Via dei Roccettini. Mon–Fri 9am–5.30pm, Sat 9am–12.30pm. Free. MAP P.129

Five minutes' walk northwest from San Domenico stands the Badìa Fiesolana, Fiesole's **cathedral** from the ninth century to the beginning of the eleventh. Tradition has it that the building stands on the spot on which St Romulus was martyred during the reign of Domitian. Cosimo il Vecchio had the church altered in the 1460s, a project which left the magnificent Romanesque facade embedded in the rough stone frontage while the interior was transformed into a superb Renaissance building – the design is based on one

THE BADIA FIESOLANA

drawn up by Brunelleschi. The monastic complex is now home to the European University Institute, an elite postgraduate research unit.

THE VILLA PEYRON

Via di Vincigliata 2, Bosco di Fontelucente 🌐 bardinipeyron.it. May–July, Sept & Oct Fri–Sun 10am–6pm. €10. Bus #47 from Fiesole. MAP P.129

Garden aficionados shouldn't miss out on the Villa Peyron, which is located 2.5km east of Fiesole. The villa itself – one of many that stud the hills around Fiesole – is open only to large pre-booked groups of 10–20 people, and is not especially fascinating anyway, but the **garden** – comprising a sequence of formal terraces surrounded by a woodland park – is a delight. Laid out by textile magnate Angelo Peyron and his son Paolo in the early years of the twentieth century, it's fed by the waters of the Fontelucente spring, hence the plethora of fountains and the pair of miniature lakes, one of which is landscaped in quasi-Japanese style. Fine views of Florence add a nice garnish to the experience.

Restaurants

LA REGGIA DEGLI ETRUSCHI

Via San Francesco 18 ☎ 055 59 385. 🌐 lareggiadeglietruschi.com. Daily 11am–3pm & 6–11pm. MAP P.129

As you'd expect, Fiesole has a few restaurants to cater for the day-trippers from Florence, but none is better than this place – the food is fine (main courses around €20), but what makes the place really memorable is the view from its dining rooms and terraces.

TERRAZZA 45

Piazza Mino da Fiesole 45 ☎ 055 597 259, 🌐 www.terrazza45.it. Daily 7–11pm, plus Sun noon–2.30pm. MAP P.129

Run by a young and very hospitable team, *Terrazza 45* is a relative newcomer to Fiesole, but it has quickly established an excellent reputation. You can eat in the stylishly monochrome dining-room or, in summer, on the panoramic terrace. Emphasis is inevitably on meat (try the pasta with wild boar), but with a few surprises, such as fried *baccalà*. Main courses around €15.

ACCOMMODATION

Hotels and residenze

Demand for accommodation in Florence is almost limitless, which means that prices are high and some hoteliers less than scrupulous. There's rarely a let-up in the tourist invasion: "low season" is officially the period from mid-November to mid-March (except for Christmas and New Year), plus the weeks from mid-July to the end of August, but any time between March and October you should book your room well in advance. The tourist office opposite the train station can find you a hotel (for a fee), but you'd be ill-advised to roll into town without having somewhere already sorted out. If none of our recommended places has a room, search the listings on the official tourism website ⓦ www.firenzeturismo.it. Never respond to the touts who hang around the train station: their hotels are likely to be expensive, or remote, or unlicensed private houses. Hotel prices in Florence are higher than anywhere else in Tuscany, but many places reduce their rates considerably in low season – and with the recession, online special discounts are becoming commonplace even in summer. The prices we've given are the quoted rates for a standard double in low and high season; bear in mind that many hotels require a two-night-minimum booking in high season. To be classified as a hotel in Florence, a building has to have at least seven bedrooms. Places with fewer rooms operate as *affitacamere* ("rooms for rent") or *residenze d'epoca* (if occupying a historic building) – though, confusingly, a *residenza d'epoca* might have as many as a dozen rooms. Some *affitacamere* are just a couple of rooms in a private house, but several – and most *residenze d'epoca* – are small hotels in all but name, offering some of the most atmospheric accommodation in Florence. Many *affitacamere* are on the upper floors of large buildings, and can be reached only by stairs.

City centre

ALDINI > Via dei Calzaiuoli 13
ⓣ 055 214 752, ⓦ hotelaldini.com.
MAP P.32, POCKET MAP C10. The rooms are somewhat functional but this two-star could hardly be more centrally placed. All fourteen rooms have private bathrooms and a/c. €60–90

BAVARIA > Borgo degli Albizi 26
ⓣ 055 234 0313, ⓦ hotelbavariafirenze.it. MAP P.32, POCKET MAP D11. A simple

Our top hotels and residenze

For a damn-the-cost weekend: *Helvetia & Bristol* p.135
For a romantic break: *Morandi alla Crocetta* p.138
For luxury on a budget: *Antica Dimora Firenze* p.137
For peace and quiet: *Torre di Bellosguardo* p.140
For a touch of history: *Brunelleschi* p.135 or *Loggiato dei Serviti* p.138
The best in Oltrarno: *Palazzo Guadagni* p.140
If you're really watching the pennies: *Cestelli* p.136

and friendly one-star near the city centre, occupying part of a sixteenth-century palazzo. Has just nine rooms, including some palatial chambers on the upper floor, and several inexpensive rooms with shared bathroom. Be sure to book, as it's popular with student tour groups. €65–105

BENIVIENI > Via delle Oche 5 ☎ 055 238 2133, ⓦ hotelbenivieni .it. MAP P.32, POCKET MAP C11. This small, family-run three-star is situated between the Duomo and Piazza della Signoria, tucked away on a quiet backstreet. Fifteen smallish rooms are ranged around two floors of a former synagogue; the rooms on the upper floor are brighter but all are simple, modern and in perfect condition. €110–220

BRUNELLESCHI > Piazza Santa Elisabetta 3 ☎ 055 27 370, ⓦ hotelbrunelleschi.it. MAP P.32, POCKET MAP C11. Designed by architect Italo Gamberini, this four-star hotel is built around a Byzantine chapel and fifth-century tower – the city's oldest building. A small in-house museum displays Roman and other fragments found during building work. Decor is simple and stylishly modern, with earthen tones predominant; the 96 rooms and suites are spacious – the best, on the fourth floor, have views of the Duomo and Campanile. €220–430

HELVETIA & BRISTOL > Via dei Pescioni 2 ☎ 055 26 651, ⓦ royaldemeure.com. MAP P.32, POCKET MAP B11. In business since 1894 and favoured by such luminaries as Pirandello, Stravinsky and Gary Cooper, this is undoubtedly Florence's finest small five-star hotel. The public spaces and 67 bedrooms and suites (each unique) are faultlessly designed and fitted, mixing antique furnishings and modern facilities – such as jacuzzis in many bathrooms – to create a style that evokes the *belle époque* without being twee. If you're going to treat yourself, this is a leading contender. €300–400

HERMITAGE > Vicolo Marzio 1/ Piazza del Pesce ☎ 055 287 216, ⓦ hermitagehotel.com. MAP P.42, POCKET MAP B13. Pre-booking is recommended year-round to secure one of the 28 rooms in this three-star hotel right next to the Ponte Vecchio, with unbeatable views from some rooms as well as from the flower-filled roof garden. The service is friendly, and rooms are cosy, decorated with the odd antique flourish; bathrooms are small but nicely done. €100–200

IL SALOTTO DI FIRENZE > Via Roma 6 ☎ 055 218 347, ⓦ ilsalottodifirenze .it. MAP P.32, POCKET MAP C10. This *residenza* has six well-appointed rooms, with three overlooking Piazza del Duomo. Perhaps not a good choice if you're a light sleeper, but the standard of accommodation is high, prices low and the location unbeatable. €100–130

MAXIM > Entrances at Via dei Calzaiuoli 11 (lift) and Via de' Medici 4 (stairs) ☎ 055 217 474, ⓦ hotelmaximfirenze.it. MAP P.32, POCKET MAP C11. Few two-star hotels offer a better location than this friendly 26-room place just a minute from the Duomo. The clean double rooms are excellent value, and all have en-suite bathrooms; the quietest look onto a central courtyard. €65–120

Renting an apartment

The high cost of hotel rooms in Florence makes **self-catering** an attractive option – for the price of a week in a cramped double room in a three-star hotel you could book yourself a two-bedroom apartment right in the centre of the city. Many package-holiday companies have a few apartments in their brochures, but a trawl of the internet will throw up dozens of places at more reasonable prices. One of the best places to look is ⓦ homeaway.co.uk, a site which puts you in touch directly with the owners and features dozens of properties in Florence.

RESIDENZA DEI PUCCI > Via dei Pucci 9 ⓣ 055 281 886, ⓦ www .residenzadeipucci.com. MAP P.32, POCKET MAP E4. Located very close to the Duomo, the *Residenza dei Pucci* occupies a fine nineteenth-century townhouse, and offers six beautifully furnished and airy rooms, each of them different from all the others. €90–150

RESIDENZA D'EPOCA IN PIAZZA DELLA SIGNORIA > Via dei Magazzini 2 ⓣ 055 239 9546, ⓦ inpiazzadellasignoria.com. MAP P.42, POCKET MAP D12. This luxurious *residenza d'epoca* has ten spacious bedrooms, several of them giving a view of the piazza. The style is antique, but tastefully restrained, and the management is very friendly. €250–280

SAVOY > Piazza della Repubblica 7 ⓣ 055 27 351, ⓦ hotelsavoy.it. MAP P.32, POCKET MAP C11. Fitted out in discreetly luxurious modern style, with plenty of bare wood, stone-coloured fabrics and peat-coloured marble, the *Savoy* is one of the city's very best hotels. Some might find it a bit too business-like, but the efficiency of the operation is impressive. And the location could not be better. €300–530

West of the centre

ALESSANDRA > Borgo Santi Apostoli 17 ⓣ 055 283 438, ⓦ hotelalessandra .com. MAP P.60–61, POCKET MAP B13. An unpretentious and very good two-star, with 27 rooms (nearly all with bathroom) occupying a sixteenth-century palazzo and furnished in a mixture of antique and modern styles. Not the cheapest two-star in town, but among the most comfortable. €150

BEACCI TORNABUONI > Via de' Tornabuoni 3 ⓣ 055 212 645, ⓦ tornabuonihotels.com. MAP P.60–61, POCKET MAP A12. With 28 individually decorated rooms occupying the top two floors of conjoined fifteenth-century palazzi, this antiques-stuffed four-star hotel offers the best value for money on Florence's poshest shopping street, with particularly good rates in the off-season. €120–230

BRETAGNA > Lungarno Corsini 6 ⓣ 055 289 618, ⓦ hotelbretagna.net. MAP P.60–61, POCKET MAP C6. This three-star riverfront hotel has a superb location and Rococo-style breakfast and living rooms. Six of the 24 rooms overlook the Arno, and most of the rest have en-suite bathrooms and a/c. €90–160

CESTELLI > Borgo SS Apostoli 25 ⓣ 055 214 213, ⓦ hotelcestelli .com. MAP P.60–61, POCKET MAP A12. Spotlessly maintained by its young Florentine–Japanese owners, this eight-roomed one-star occupies part of a house that once belonged to a minor Medici, whose bust adorns the facade. The rooms are a good size, and most are en suite. €70–100

ELITE Via della Scala 12 ⓣ 055 215 395, ⓦ hotelelitefirenze.com. MAP P.60–61, POCKET MAP C4. Of all the hotels on this street, the ten-room two-star *Elite* is the real bargain. It's basic but clean and is run by a very pleasant management. Most rooms have private bathrooms; ask for a room at the back, as Via della Scala is quite a busy road. €45–70

GALLERY HOTEL ART > Vicolo dell'Oro 5 ☎ 055 27 263, Ⓦ lungarnohotels .com. MAP P.60–61, POCKET MAP B13. In a small, quiet square a few paces from the Ponte Vecchio, this immensely stylish four-star is unlike any other hotel in central Florence. Owned by the Ferragamo fashion house, it has a sleek, minimalist and hyper-modern look – lots of dark wood and neutral colours – and tasteful contemporary art displayed in the reception and all 74 rooms. There's a small but smart bar, a sushi restaurant and an attractive lounge with art-filled bookshelves and comfortable sofas. €250–300

J.K. PLACE > Piazza Santa Maria Novella 7 ☎ 055 264 5181, Ⓦ jkplace.com. MAP P.60–61, POCKET MAP C5. One of the most appealing of Florence's designer hotels occupies a fine eighteenth-century building on Piazza Santa Maria Novella. The twenty rooms of this elegant townhouse have been designed by Michele Bönan in retro-modernist hybrid style, and have DVD players and flat-screen TVs. €320–400

NIZZA > Via del Giglio 5 ☎ 055 239 6897, Ⓦ hotelnizza.com. MAP P.60–61, POCKET MAP A10. A smart eighteen-room family-run two star, with helpful staff and very central location. All rooms are en suite, and are better furnished and decorated than many in this category. €60–110

PORTA ROSSA > Via Porta Rossa 19 ☎ 055 271 0911, Ⓦ nh-hotels .com. MAP P.60–61, POCKET MAP A12. Florence's most venerable four-star hotel, the 72-room *Porta Rossa* has been in business since the beginning of the nineteenth century and has hosted, among others, Byron and Stendhal. Recently reopened after a long renovation, it retains something of its old ambience while the rooms have been fitted out in crisp but luxuriously modern style, with red and white the dominant tones. €170–385

TORRE GUELFA > Borgo SS Apostoli 8 ☎ 055 239 6338, Ⓦ hoteltorreguelfa .com. MAP P.60–61, POCKET MAP B12. Twenty tastefully furnished rooms are crammed into the third floor of this ancient tower, the tallest private building in the city; there are marvellous views from the small roof garden. There are also six cheaper doubles on the first floor (no TV and more noise from the road). Though slightly shabby in places, this is a characterful hotel, and very popular. €100–200

North of the centre

ANTICA DIMORA FIRENZE > Via San Gallo 72 ☎ 055 462 7296, Ⓦ johanna .it. MAP P.76–77, POCKET MAP F2. This plush *residenza*, run by the owners of the neighbouring *Antica Dimora Johlea* and *Residenza Johlea* (see below), has six very comfortable double rooms, some with four-poster beds. €160

ANTICA DIMORA JOHLEA > Via San Gallo 80 ☎ 055 461 185, Ⓦ johanna.it. MAP P.76–77, POCKET MAP F2. Slightly pricier and a little more luxurious than the *Antica Dimora Firenze* (see above), this lovely *residenza* also has a nice roof terrace, giving a roofline view of the Duomo and the hills beyond. €170

AZZI > Via Faenza 56 ☎ 055 213 806, Ⓦ hotelazzi.com. MAP P.76–77, POCKET MAP D4. This immensely welcoming three-star has fifteen bedrooms decorated in a cosily rustic style, with antique furnishings and garden views from most rooms. The owners are keen musicians, and at 7pm on Thursdays they put on a song recital for guests, with *aperitivi*. €50–120

CASCI > Via Cavour 13 ☎ 055 211 686, Ⓦ hotelcasci.com. MAP P.76–77, POCKET MAP E4. It would be hard to find a more hospitable two-star in central Florence than this 26-room family-run hotel, which occupies part of a building in which Rossini once stayed. Only two (sound-proofed) rooms face the busy street; the rest are very quiet, and all are clean and neat, if somewhat compact. The welcome is unfailingly warm, the owners are immensely helpful, and the buffet breakfast – laid out under the frescoed ceiling of the reception area – is generous. **€90–150**

GLOBUS > Via Sant'Antonino 24 ☎ 055 211 062, Ⓦ hotelglobus.com. MAP P.76–77, POCKET MAP D4. Located right by San Lorenzo church, the *Globus* has a refreshingly different style from most of Florence's three-stars – wenge wood furniture and natural tones predominate, rather than the usual antiques and chintz. **€80–180**

KURSAAL AUSONIA > Via Nazionale 24 ☎ 055 496 324, Ⓦ kursonia. com. MAP P.76–77, POCKET MAP D3. Welcoming, recently refurbished three-star near the station, with accommodation ranging from spacious "superior" doubles, in faux-antique style, to rather more bland and functional "standard" rooms. **€60–120**

LOCANDA DEI POETI > Via Guelfa 74 ☎ 055 488 701, Ⓦ locandadeipoeti .com. MAP P.76–77, POCKET MAP D3. Run by an actor and his partner, this small B&B has a poetry theme, as you might have guessed. Various parts of the building are dedicated to different poets, and poems are written on some of the walls. The wackiness doesn't extend to the four individually styled bedrooms, however. **€50–200**

LOGGIATO DEI SERVITI > Piazza Santissima Annunziata 3 ☎ 055 289 592, Ⓦ loggiatodeiservitihotel .it. MAP P.76–77, POCKET MAP F3. Elegant three-star in one of Florence's most celebrated squares. Its 38 rooms have been incorporated into a structure designed in the sixteenth century in imitation of the Brunelleschi hospital across the square, to accommodate the Servite priests who worked there. The plainness of some rooms reflects something of the building's history, but all are decorated with fine fabrics and antiques, and look out either onto the piazza or peaceful gardens to the rear: top-floor rooms have glimpses of the Duomo. The five rooms in the nearby annexe, at Via dei Servi 49, are similarly styled, but the building doesn't have the same charisma. **€150–180**

MERLINI > Via Faenza 56 ☎ 055 212 848, Ⓦ hotelmerlini.it. MAP P.76–77, POCKET MAP D3. Several budget hotels are crammed into this address, and the family-run *Merlini*, on the third floor (no lift), is one of the best. Its ten rooms have marble bathrooms – an unexpected bonus in this price bracket – and six give views of the Duomo. **€60–110**

MORANDI ALLA CROCETTA > Via Laura 50 ☎ 055 234 4747, Ⓦ hotelmorandi.it. MAP P.76–77, POCKET MAP G3. An intimate three-star gem, whose small size and friendly welcome ensure a home-from-home atmosphere. Rooms are tastefully decorated with antiques and old prints, and vivid carpets laid on parquet floors. Two rooms have balconies opening onto a modest garden; another – with fresco fragments and medieval nooks and crannies – was converted from the site's former convent chapel. **€110–170**

MR. MY RESORT > Via delle Ruote 14a ☎ 055 283 955, Ⓦ mrflorence.it. MAP P.76–77, POCKET MAP E2. Run by the same friendly family as *Relais Grand Tour* (see below), this luxury B&B has five bright, quirkily furnished rooms arranged around a tranquil garden, but the real draw is the private, stone-walled spa in the basement, complete with Turkish bath and jacuzzi. **€130–150**

ORTO DE' MEDICI > Via San Gallo 30 ☎ 055 483 427, Ⓦ ortodeimedici .it. MAP P.76–77, POCKET MAP E3. A 31-room frescoed and antique-furnished three-star, occupying a quiet palazzo in the university area. Via San Gallo is not the most attractive street in Florence, but the hotel has a nice formal garden and has been very impressively refurbished; its off-season rates are terrific too. **€70–190**

RELAIS GRAND TOUR > Via Santa Reparata 21 ☎ 055 283 955, Ⓦ florencegrandtour.com. MAP P.76–77, POCKET MAP E3. The very hospitable owners have done a great job in turning two floors of this old palazzo, adjoining an eighteenth-century private theatre, into a superb guesthouse, with three large bedrooms upstairs and three suites on the ground floor. Each room is unique – one suite has Neapolitan majolica tiles in the bathroom, while another (formerly a dressing-room) is loaded with antique mirrors ("suitable for a couple", as the website has it). €110–130

RESIDENZA CASTIGLIONI > Via del Giglio 8 ☎ 055 239 6013, Ⓦ residenzacastiglioni.com. MAP P.76–77, POCKET MAP D4. This discreet and hugely stylish hideaway has just half a dozen spacious en-suite double rooms (three of them frescoed), on the second floor of a palazzo very close to San Lorenzo church. Room 22 is the one to go for, with wall-to-wall frescoes. €100–150

RESIDENZA JOHANNA I > Via Bonifacio Lupi 14 ☎ 055 481 896, Ⓦ johanna.it. MAP P.76–77, POCKET MAP E2. The longest-established of the *Johanna/Johlea* family of *residenze*, this genteel place is hidden away in an unmarked apartment building in a quiet, leafy corner of the city, a 5min walk north of San Marco. Rooms are cosy and well kept, and the management are as friendly and helpful as you could hope for. €130

RESIDENZA JOHANNA II > Via Cinque Giornate 12 ☎ 055 473 377, Ⓦ johanna.it. MAP P.76–77, POCKET MAP D1. The location of this *residenza* – to the north of the Fortezza da Basso – is a little less convenient than that of its siblings, but the accommodation is of the same high standard, as is the hospitality. €110

RESIDENZA JOHLEA > Via San Gallo 76 ☎ 055 463 3292, Ⓦ johanna.it. MAP P.76–77, POCKET MAP F2. Another property from the portfolio of the owners of *Residenza Johanna* (see above), offering the same low-cost, high-comfort package. €130

East of the centre

DALÌ > Via dell' Oriuolo 17 ☎ 055 234 0706, Ⓦ hoteldali.com. MAP P.94–95, POCKET MAP F5. One of the least expensive one-star options close to the centre, with just nine rooms, five

with bath. The rooms are plain and rather basic, but the location – on the top floor of a palazzo built in 1492 – helps, as does the view from the back rooms of the giant magnolia in the garden below. The friendly owners speak good English. €70–90

J & J > Via di Mezzo 20 ☎ 055 263 12, Ⓦ jandjhotel.net. MAP P.94–95, POCKET MAP G5. The bland exterior of this former fifteenth-century convent conceals a romantic nineteen-room four-star hotel. Some rooms are vast split-level affairs, but all have charm and are furnished with modern fittings and a few antiques. Common areas are decked with flowers, and retain frescoes and vaulted ceilings from the original building. In summer, breakfast is served in the convent's lovely old cloister. €150–210

RELAIS SANTA CROCE > Via Ghibellina 87 ☎ 055 234 2230, Ⓦ relaisantacroce.com. MAP P.94–95, POCKET MAP F6. This magnificent five-star shares a lobby with the mind-blowingly expensive *Pinchiorri* restaurant, and is a similarly top-flight establishment. The grandiose public rooms are a very slick amalgam of the historic and the contemporary, with modern sofas set on acres of gleaming parquet, surrounded by eighteenth-century stucco panels. Contemporary and understated luxury prevails in the bedrooms, which are graded "superior", "deluxe" and "exclusive" (these have their own saunas). Then there are suites, which are in the "if you have to ask the price you can't afford it" category. €250–450

Oltrarno

ANNALENA > Via Romana 34 ☎ 055 222 402, Ⓦ annalenahotel.com. MAP P.106–107, POCKET MAP B8. A short way beyond Palazzo Pitti (and right by an entrance to the Bóboli gardens), this bargain twenty-room three-star occupies part of a building once owned by the Medici. The best rooms open onto a gallery with garden views, and a sprinkling of antiques lends a hint of old-world charm. €80–120

LA SCALETTA > Via Guicciardini 13 ☎ 055 283 028, ⓦ lascaletta.com. MAP P.106–107, POCKET MAP D7. Some of the rooms in this tidy and recently refurbished sixteen-room three-star give views across to the Bóboli gardens; those on the Via Guicciardini side are double-glazed against the traffic. Drinks are served on the rooftop terraces, where you look across the Bóboli in one direction and the city in the other. All rooms are en suite and nicely decorated in creamy tones. €60–120

PALAZZO GUADAGNI > Piazza Santo Spirito 9 ☎ 055 265 8376, ⓦ palazzoguadagni.com. MAP P.106–107, POCKET MAP C7. This very attractive

three-star hotel has 15 rooms on three floors, furnished with family antiques. The middle floor is nicest, particularly room 10, with its frescoed ceiling. The lovely loggia gets the evening sun – the perfect place to wind down with an *aperitivo*. €100–140

TORRE DI BELLOSGUARDO > Via Roti Michelozzi 2 ☎ 055 229 8145, ⓦ torrebellosguardo.com. MAP P.106–107, POCKET MAP A8. It's not central – it's perched on a hill about 2km from the heart of Oltrarno – but the four-star *Bellosguardo* is one of the most beautiful hotels in the city. Dating back to the thirteenth century, it's girdled by magnificent gardens (with a pool), and each of its 16 rooms (each uniquely and exquisitely furnished) is palatial. €230–290

Hostels

ACADEMY HOSTEL > Via Ricasoli 9 ☎ 055 239 8665, ⓦ academyhostel .eu. MAP P.32, POCKET MAP E4. Since opening in 2008, this modern hostel has won awards for its service and excellent facilities: set in a seventeenth-century palazzo, it offers airy, high-ceilinged rooms (from singles to 6 beds) and a common area with huge flat-screen TV, book and DVD library and lots of computer terminals, plus a sunny terrace. All this, and an unbeatable location – just steps from the Duomo. Breakfast included. Price per person per night from €30

ARCHI ROSSI > Via Faenza 94r ☎ 055 290 804, ⓦ hostelarchirossi.com. MAP P.76–77, POCKET MAP D3. A 5min walk from the train station, this privately owned hostel is spotlessly clean and decorated with guests' wall-paintings and

graffiti. It's popular – the 140 beds fill up quickly – and has a pleasant garden and terrace. There are some basic en-suite doubles too (on the third floor; no lift), and a restaurant serving cheap meals. Breakfast included. Dorm beds from €22, single rooms from €40

FORESTERIA VALDESE FIRENZE – ISTITUTO GOULD > Via dei Serragli 49 ☎ 055 212 576, ⓦ istitutogould .it. MAP P.106–107, POCKET MAP B7. Run by the Waldensian Church, this hostel-cum-evangelical college occupies part of a seventeenth-century palazzo between Santo Spirito and the Carmine. The 99 beds (in 39 rooms) are extremely popular, so book in advance, especially during the academic year. Street-front rooms can be noisy (rear rooms cost a little more), but the old courtyard, terracotta floors and stone staircases

The Area di Sosta

When the Florence campsites are full (which in summer they often are), the city authorities sometimes set aside an Area di Sosta, an emergency accommodation area which usually amounts to a patch of ground sheltered by a rudimentary roof, with a shower block attached. Contact the tourist offices for details, if any, of the current location.

provide atmosphere throughout. Check-in Mon–Fri 8.45am–1pm & 3–7.30pm, Sat 9am–1.30pm & 2.30–6pm; reception closed Sun. No curfew. **Dorm beds from €20, single rooms from €45**

SANTA MONACA > Via Santa Monaca 6 ☏ 055 268 338, Ⓦ ostello. it. MAP P.106–107, POCKET MAP B6. This privately owned hostel in Oltrarno has 112 beds, arranged in a dozen dorms (female-only and mixed) with between two and twenty beds. Kitchen facilities, laundry and free internet; meals are available but are not included. Check-in 6am–2am; lock-out 10am–2pm. Curfew 2am. It's a 10min walk from the station, or take bus #11, #36 or #37 to the second stop after the bridge. **Dorm beds from €16**

VILLA CAMERATA > Viale Augusto Righi 2–4 ☏ 055 601 451, Ⓦ ostellofirenze.it. Buses #17 and #17b from the station. MAP P.125, POCKET MAP H2. This HI hostel in a beautiful park 5km northeast of the city is one of Europe's most attractive hostels, a sixteenth-century house with frescoed ceilings. There are 320 beds, and a few private rooms. Films in English are shown every night. Breakfast is included, but there are no kitchen facilities; dinner costs around €12. Check-in from 2pm. **Dorm beds from €18**

Campsites

CAMPING MICHELANGELO > Viale Michelangiolo 80 ☏ 055 681 1977, Ⓦ camping.it/toscana/Michelangelo. Bus #13 from the train station. MAP P.108–109, POCKET MAP H9. A 240-pitch site that's always crowded, owing to its superb hillside location in an olive grove overlooking the city centre. It has kitchen facilities and a well-stocked, if expensive, shop nearby. Open all year. **From €9.50 per person, pitches from €12.50**

CAMPING PANORAMICO > Via Peramondo 1, Fiesole ☏ 055 559 069, Ⓦ www.florencecamping.com.

MAP P.129, POCKET MAP H1. Located in Fiesole, this 120-pitch three-star site has a bar, restaurant, pool and small supermarket. Mid-March to Dec. **From €10 per person, plus €6.50 per tent**

VILLA CAMERATA > Viale Augusto Righi 2–4 ☏ 055 601 451, Ⓦ ostellofirenze.it. Buses #17 and #17b from the station. MAP P.125, POCKET MAP H2. A basic 55-pitch campsite in the grounds of the HI hostel, open year-round. **From €8 per person, plus €6 per tent**

Arrival

Your point of arrival is most likely to be Santa Maria Novella train station, which is located within a few minutes' walk of the heart of the historic centre: rail and bus connections from the three airports that serve the city all terminate at the station, as do international trains and buses from all over Italy.

Pisa airport

Most flights to Tuscany use Pisa's **Galileo Galilei** airport (☏050 849 300, ⊕pisa-airport.com), 95km west of Florence and 3km from the centre of Pisa. Terravision shuttle **buses** are scheduled to synchronize with incoming budget-airline flights and leave from in front of the terminal; they take seventy minutes to reach Florence's Santa Maria Novella station, and tickets (€7 single) are sold at the stand right in front of you as you come out into the airport concourse. **Trains** from the airport station cost €7.80 and are often slower (70–100min in total, depending on connections at Pisa Centrale); there are only eight direct trains daily (6.50am–10pm), but every thirty minutes a shuttle train runs from the airport to Pisa Centrale (5min), where you can change to one of the hourly services to Florence (journey time 1hr). Train tickets can be bought from the office at the opposite end of the concourse from machines on the station platforms. Remember to validate your ticket in the platform machine before boarding the train. If you're arriving very late, you'll have to take the five-minute bus, train or taxi ride to Pisa Centrale, from where trains to Florence start running from around 6.30am.

Perètola airport

A few airlines use Florence's small Perètola (Amerigo Vespucci) airport (☏055 306 1300, ⊕aeroporto.firenze.it), 5km northwest of the city centre. The SITA and ATAF bus companies operate a joint service from Perètola called Volainbus (⊕ataf.net), which provides half-hourly shuttles into the city from immediately outside the arrivals area. Tickets can be bought on board or from machines at the airport, and the journey takes about thirty minutes.

Bologna airport

A few airlines use Bologna (⊕bologna-airport.it) as a gateway airport for Florence. Aerobus shuttles depart every twenty minutes (7.30am–11.45pm) from outside the airport's Terminal A to Bologna's main train station (about 25min), from where regular trains run to Florence's Santa Maria Novella station in about an hour. Note, however, that Ryanair services to Bologna in fact fly to Forlì airport, which is more than 60km southeast of Bologna, and very inconvenient for Florence.

The train station

Florence's central station, Santa Maria Novella ("Firenze SMN" on timetables), is located just north of the church and square of Santa Maria Novella, a couple of blocks west of the Duomo. In the station are an accommodation service, left-luggage facilities and a 24-hour pharmacy. While in and around the station, you should keep a close eye on your bags at all times: it's a prime hunting-ground for thieves and pickpockets. Also avoid the concourse's various taxi and hotel touts, however friendly they may appear.

Getting around

Within the historic centre, walking is generally the most efficient way of getting around, and nowadays walking is a lot more pleasant than it used to be, with the extension of the **zona a traffico limitato** (ZTL) – which limits traffic in the centre to residents' cars, delivery vehicles and public transport – to cover most of the city centre from the river to a few blocks north of the Duomo.

Buses

If you want to cross town in a hurry, or visit some of the peripheral sights, your best option is to use one of the frequent and speedy orange **ATAF** buses (www.ataf.net). Tickets are valid for unlimited journeys within a period of 90min (€1.20; €2 if bought on-board), 24hr (€5), 72hr (€12) or seven days (€18). A **Biglietto Multiplo** gives four 90min tickets for €4.70. Much better value is the ATAF electronic card called the **Carnet Agile**, which comes in three versions: the €10 card gives the equivalent of ten 90min tickets; the €20 card is equivalent to 21; and the €30 card is equivalent to 35. You can buy tickets from the main ATAF office outside Santa Maria Novella station (Mon–Sat 7.30am–7.30pm), from any shops and stalls displaying the ATAF sign, and from automatic machines all over Florence. Once you're on board, you must validate your ticket or card at the start of every journey. There's a hefty on-the-spot fine for any passenger without a validated ticket.

Taxis

You can't flag down a taxi in the street – you have to phone for one (☎055 4242, ☎055 4798, ☎055 4499 or ☎055 4390) or go to a taxi rank; key locations include the train station, Piazza della Repubblica, Piazza del Duomo, Piazza Santa Maria Novella, Piazza San Marco, Piazza Santa Croce and Piazza Santa Trinita. If you order a cab by phone, you'll be given the car's code name – usually a town, city or country – and its number, both of which are emblazoned on the vehicle. All rides are metered; at the start of the journey the meter should be set at €3.30, €5.30 if it's a Sunday or public holiday, or €6.60 between 10pm and 6am. Supplements are payable for journeys outside the city limits (to Fiesole, for example), and for each piece of luggage placed in the boot (€0.60).

The Tramvia

The first line of the city's controversial Tramvia tram system line – line T1, a commuter service from Santa Maria Novella to Scandicci – was completed in 2010. Line T2 was originally intended to go from Perètola airport to Piazza della Libertà, via Piazza del Duomo, but its route is now being reassessed. It was scheduled for completion in 2014, but financial problems have delayed it, and might in the end kill it off, along with the planned T3, which is meant to go from Careggi (north of the city centre) to Santa Maria Novella, possibly with an extension to Bagno a Ripoli in the southeast.

Directory A–Z

Banks

Florence's main bank branches are on or around Piazza della Repubblica, but exchange booths (*cambio*) and ATM cash-card machines (*bancomat*) for Visa and MasterCard advances can be found across the city. Banks generally open Mon–Fri 8.20am–3.35pm.

Consulates

The UK consulate for northern Italy is at Via San Paolo 7, Milan ☎02 723 001; the US has a consulate in Florence, at Lungarno Amerigo Vespucci 38 ☎055 266 951.

Electricity

The supply in Italy is 220V, but anything requiring 240V will work. Most plugs have two round pins, so UK equipment will need an adapter. US equipment requires a transformer as well.

Emergencies

Police ☎113, or ☎112 for the Carabinieri (military police); fire ☎115; ambulance ☎118. If your passport is lost or stolen, go to the police (see opposite) and report it to your consulate.

Health

The Medical Service is a private service used to dealing with foreigners; they have doctors on call 24hr a day on ☎055 475 411 (⊛medicalservice.firenze.it), or you can visit their clinic at Via Lorenzo il Magnifico 59 (Mon–Fri 11am–noon & 5–6pm, Sat 11am–noon). Note that you'll need insurance cover to recoup the cost of a consultation, which will be at least €60. Florence's central hospital is on Piazza Santa Maria Nuova.

Internet access

Internet Train (⊛internettrain.it) has branches at Via de Benci 36r, Via Porta Rossa 38r and Vial dell' Oriuolo 40r – they're open Mon–Sat 10am–midnight, Sun 3–11pm. Many hotels (and all of the pricier ones) now offer free internet access.

Left luggage

The left luggage office is at Santa Maria Novella station, by platform 16 (daily 6am–midnight).

Lost property

Lost property handed in at the city or railway police ends up at Via Veracini 5 (Mon, Wed & Fri 9am–12.30pm, Tues & Thurs 9am–12.30pm & 2.30–4.30pm; ☎055 334 802; bus #17, #29, #30 or #35).

Museum admission

All of Florence's state-run museums belong to an association called Firenze Musei (⊛www.firenzemusei.it), which sets aside a daily quota of tickets that can be reserved in advance. The Uffizi, the Accademia

Florentine addresses

Note that there is a **double address system** in Florence, one for businesses and one for all other properties – that, at least, is the theory, though in fact the distinction is far from rigorous. Business addresses are followed by the letter r (for *rosso*) and are marked on the building with a red number on a white plate, sometimes with an r after the numeral, but not always. The two series are independent of each other, which means that no. 20, for example, may be a long way from no. 20r.

Firenze Card

The Firenze Card, costing €50, is valid for 72 hours from the first time you use it, and gives access to more than 30 museums in greater Florence (including all the big ones), plus unlimited use of public transport. It also enables you to by-pass the queues, as the major museums have separate gates for card holders. You do, though, have to pack a hell of a lot into each day to make it worth the investment. The card can be bought at the Via Cavour and Piazza Stazione tourist offices, from the Uffizi, Bargello, Palazzo Pitti, Museo Bardini and Museo di Santa Maria Novella, and at ⊚firenzecard.it.

and the Bargello belong to this group, as do the Palazzo Pitti museums, the Bóboli gardens, the Medici chapels in San Lorenzo, the archeological museum and the San Marco museum. The best source of online info for all of these museums is ⊚uffizi. firenze.it.

You can **reserve tickets** (booking fee of €4 for Uffizi and Accademia, €3 for the rest) by phoning ☎055 294 883 (Mon–Fri 8.30am–6.30pm, Sat 8.30am–12.30pm), online at ⊚www. firenzemusei.it and ⊚uffizi.firenze.it, at the Firenze Musei booth at Orsanmichele (Mon–Sat 10am–5.30pm), and at the museums themselves, in the case of the Uffizi and Pitti. If you book by phone, an English-speaking operator will allocate you a ticket for a specific hour, to be collected at the museum at a specific time, shortly before entry. That's the theory, but in reality the line tends to be engaged for long periods at a stretch. Generally, the under-publicized Orsanmichele booth – which is set into the wall of the church on the Via Calzaiuoli side – is the easiest option. Pre-booking is very strongly recommended at any time of year for the Uffizi (see p.00 for more) and the Accademia, whose allocation of reservable tickets is often sold out many days ahead.

Note that on-the-door admission to all state-run museums is free for EU citizens under 18 and over 65, on presentation of a passport; 18–25s get a fifty percent discount, as do teachers, on proof of identity. Nearly all of Florence's major museums are routinely **closed on Monday**, though some are open for a couple of Mondays each month. In the majority of cases, museum ticket offices close thirty minutes before the museum itself. At the Palazzo Vecchio and Museo Stibbert, however, it's one hour before, while at the Uffizi, Bargello, Museo dell'Opera del Duomo, the dome of the Duomo, the Campanile and Pitti museums it's 45 minutes.

For Florence's civic museums – of which the main ones are the Museo Bardini, Museo Santa Maria Novella, Palazzo Vecchio and the Cappella Brancacci – the website is ⊚www .museicivicifiorentini.it.

Pharmacies

The Farmacia Comunale, on the train station concourse, is open 24hr. All'Insegna del Moro, at Piazza San Giovanni 20r, on the north side of the Baptistery, and Farmacia Molteni, at Via dei Calzaiuoli 7r, alternate their 24hr service every two weeks. All pharmacies display a late-night roster in their window.

Police

Emergency ☎112 or 113. To report a theft or other crime, go to the Carabinieri at Borgo Ognissanti 48, to the Questura at Via Zara 2

Florence online

Agenzia per il Turismo di Firenze ⓦwww.firenze.turismo.it. An official tourist office site (there are several), with an English-language option. Useful for information on forthcoming exhibitions and hotel listings.

Firenze Spettacolo ⓦfirenzespettacolo.it. The online edition of Florence's listings magazine.

Musei Civici ⓦwww.museicivicifiorentini.it. Information on Florence's civic museums.

(both 24hr), or to the tourist police at Via Pietrapiana 50r (Mon–Fri 8.30am–6.30pm, Sat closes 1pm) – you're more likely to find an English-speaker at the last of these. If you do report a theft or other crime, you will have to fill out a form (*una denuncia*); this may be time-consuming, but it's essential if you want to make a claim on your travel insurance on returning home.

Post office

The main central post office is near Piazza della Repubblica at Via Pellicceria 3 (Mon–Fri 8.25am–7.10pm, Sat 8.25am–12.35pm). If all you want are stamps (*francobolli*), then it's easier to buy them at one of the city's innumerable tabacchi, which are marked by a sign outside with a white "T" on a blue background.

Telephones

Nearly all of Florence's public call-boxes accept coins, but you get more time for your euros if you use a phone card, which can be bought from any tabacchi and any shop displaying the Telecom Italia sticker. You're never far from a pay phone – every sizeable piazza has at least one.

Time

Italy is on Central European Time (CET), one hour ahead of the UK, six hours ahead of Eastern Standard Time and nine hours ahead of Pacific Standard Time.

Tourist information

The main tourist office is at Via Cavour 1r, a 5min walk north of the Duomo (Mon–Sat 8.30am–6.30pm; ⓣ055 290 832, ⓦwww.firenze-turismo.it); this office provides information not just on the city but on the whole of Florence province. Smaller offices are in the Loggia del Bigallo, by the Baptistery (Mon–Sat 9am–7pm, Sun 9am–2pm; ⓣ055 288 496), and opposite the train station, at Piazza della Stazione 4 (Mon–Sat 8.30am–7pm, Sun 8.30am–2pm; ⓣ055 212 245).

All three provide an adequate **map** and various leaflets, including a sheet with updated opening hours and entrance charges, and the office at Via Cavour also handles information on the whole of Florence province. Another excellent source of information is *Firenze Spettacolo* (ⓦfirenzespettacolo.it; €2), a monthly, mostly bilingual listings magazine available from bookshops and larger newsstands. Also useful is *The Florentine* (ⓦtheflorentine.net) a free bi-weekly English-language paper, available at the tourist office, most bookshops and various other spots (the website lists all of the places it can be picked up).

Festivals and events

SCOPPIO DEL CARRO

Easter Sunday

For Easter Sunday's Scoppio del Carro (Explosion of the Cart) a cartload of fireworks is hauled by six white oxen from the Porta a Prato to the Duomo; there, during the midday Mass, the whole lot is set off by a "dove" that whizzes down a wire from the high altar.

FESTA DEL GRILLO

First Sunday after Ascension

On the first Sunday after Ascension Day (forty days after Easter), the Festa del Grillo (Festival of the Cricket) is held in the Cascine park. In among the market stalls and the picnickers, people sell tiny mechanical crickets. Live crickets were sold until recently, a vestige of a ritual that may hark back to the days when farmers had to scour their land for locusts.

MAGGIO MUSICALE FIORENTINO

May–June

ⓦmaggiofiorentino.com

Confusingly, the Maggio Musicale isn't restricted to May (Maggio), but lasts for a couple of months from late April or early May. The festival has its own orchestra, chorus and ballet company, plus guest appearances from foreign ensembles. Events are staged at the Teatro Comunale (or its Teatro Piccolo), the Teatro della Pergola, the Palazzo dei Congressi, the Teatro Verdi, the new opera house and occasionally in the Bóboli gardens. Information and tickets can be obtained from the Teatro Comunale, Corso Italia 16.

ESTATE FIESOLANA

June–August

ⓦwww.estatefiesolana.it

Slightly less exclusive than the Maggio Musicale (see above), concentrating more on chamber and symphonic music, the Estate Fiesolana is held in Fiesole every summer, usually from June to late August. Films and theatre are also featured, and most events are held in the open-air Teatro Romano.

ST JOHN'S DAY AND THE CALCIO STORICO

June 24 and two later dates

The saint's day of John the Baptist, Florence's patron, is June 24 – the occasion for a massive fireworks display up on Piazzale Michelangelo, and for the first game of the Calcio Storico. Played in sixteenth-century costume, this uniquely Florentine mayhem is a three-match series played on June 24 and two subsequent dates later in the month or in early July (they change from year to year), with fixtures nearly always being held in Piazza Santa Croce. Each of the four historic quarters fields a team of 27 players, Santa Croce playing in blue, San Giovanni in green, Santa Maria Novella in red and Santo Spirito in impractical white. The prize for the winning side is a vast quantity of steak, equivalent to the white calf traditionally awarded to the victors.

FESTA DELLE RIFICOLONE

September 7

The Festa delle Rificolone (Festival of the Lanterns) takes place on the Virgin's birthday, September 7, with a procession of children to Piazza Santissima Annunziata, where market stalls are set out for the evening. Each child carries a coloured paper lantern with a candle inside it – a throwback to the days when people from the surrounding countryside would troop by lantern light into the city for the Feast of the Virgin.

National holidays

Everything, except some bars and restaurants, closes on Italy's official **national holidays**, which are: January 1, January 6 (Epiphany), Easter Monday, April 25 (Liberation Day), May 1 (Labour Day), June 2 (Day of the Republic), August 15 (Ferragosto; Assumption), November 1 (Ognissanti; All Saints), December 8 (Immaculate Conception), December 25, December 26.

Chronology

Eighth century BC > The Etruscans are settled throughout the area known as Tuscany, with their principal settlements in Roselle, Vetulonia, Populonia, Volterra, Chiusi, Cortona, Arezzo and – most northerly of all – Fiesole.

59 BC > The Roman colony of Florentia is established by Julius Caesar as a settlement for army veterans. By now the Romans have either subsumed or exterminated most Etruscan towns.

Second and third centuries AD > Rapid expansion of Florentia as a river port.

Fourth century AD > Christianity is spreading throughout Italy. The church of San Lorenzo and the martyr's shrine at San Miniato are both established in Florentia.

552 > Florence falls to the hordes of the Gothic king Totila. Less than twenty years later the Lombards storm in, subjugating the city to the duchy whose capital was in Pavia.

End of the eighth century > Charlemagne's Franks have taken control of much of Italy, with the administration overseen by imperial margraves, based in Lucca. These proxy rulers develop into some of the most powerful figures in the Holy Roman Empire and are instrumental in spreading Christianity even further.

978 > Willa, widow of the margrave Uberto, establishes the Badìa in Florence, the first monastic foundation in the centre of the city.

1027 > The position of margrave passes to the Canossa family, who take the title of the Counts of Tuscia (as Tuscany was then called). The most influential figure produced by this dynasty is Matilda, daughter of the first Canossa margrave.

1115 > In the year of Matilda's death she grants Florence the status of an independent city. The new commune of Florence is essentially governed by a council of one hundred men, the great majority drawn from the rising merchant class. In 1125 the city's increasing dominance of the region is confirmed when it crushes the rival city of Fiesole. Fifty years later, as the population booms with the rise of the textile industry, new walls are built around what is now one of the largest cities in Europe.

Thirteenth century > Throughout Tuscany, conflict develops between the Ghibelline faction and the Guelphs – the former, broadly speaking, are pro-empire, with the Guelphs defined chiefly by their loyalty to the papacy. When Charles of Anjou conquers Naples in 1266, association with the anti-imperial French becomes another component of Guelphism, and a loose Guelph alliance soon stretches from Paris to Naples, substantially funded by the bankers of Tuscany. Florence and Lucca are generally Guelph strongholds, while Pisa, Arezzo, Prato, Pistoia and Siena tend to side with the empire.

1207 > Florence's governing council is replaced by the *podestà*, an executive official who is traditionally a non-Florentine. Around this time the first *arti* (guilds) are formed to promote the interests of the traders and bankers.

1248 > Florence's Ghibellines enlist the help of Emperor Frederick II to oust the Guelphs, but within two years they have been displaced by the Guelph-backed regime of the Primo Popolo, a quasi-democratic government drawn from the mercantile class.

1280 > Power passes to the Secondo Popolo, a regime run by the Arti Maggiori (Great Guilds). The fulcrum of power in Florence shifts definitively towards its bankers, merchants and manufacturers.

1293 > The Secondo Popolo excludes the nobility from government and invests power in the Signoria, a council drawn from the Arti Maggiori.

1348 > The Black Death destroys as many as half the city's population. However, the plague is equally devastating throughout the region, and does nothing to reverse the economic and political supremacy of the city.

1406 > Florence takes control of Pisa and thus gains a long-coveted seaport. Despite the survival of Sienese independence into the sixteenth century, the history of Tuscany increasingly becomes the history of Florence.

1431–1434 > Cosimo de' Medici is imprisoned by the city authorities, having provoked the big families of the Signoria with his support for the members of the disenfranchised lesser guilds. In 1434, after a session of the Parlamento – a general council called in times of emergency – he is invited to return.

Having secured the military support of the Sforza family of Milan, Cosimo (Cosimo il Vecchio) becomes the pre-eminent figure in the city's political life for more than three decades. Florence's reputation as the most innovative cultural centre in Europe is strengthened by his patronage of Donatello, Michelozzo and a host of other artists.

1439 > Council of Florence is convened, to try to reconcile the Catholic and Eastern churches. The consequent influx of Greek scholars adds momentum to the study of classical philosophy and literature.

1478 > The Pazzi family conspire with Pope Sixtus IV to murder Lorenzo il Magnifico (Cosimo's grandson, and the de facto ruler of Florence) and his brother Giuliano; the plot fails, and only increases the esteem in which Lorenzo is held.

1494 > Lorenzo's son Piero is obliged to flee Florence following his surrender to the invading French army of Charles VIII. This invasion is the commencement of a bloody half-century dominated by the so-called Wars of Italy.

1498 > Having in effect ruled the city in the absence of the Medici, the Dominican friar Girolamo Savonarola is executed as a heretic.

1512 > Following Florence's defeat by the Spanish and papal armies, the Medici return, in the person of the vicious Giuliano, Duke of Nemours.

1527 > Holy Roman Emperor Charles V's army pillages Rome. The humiliation of Pope Clement VII (a Medici) spurs the people of Florence to eject his deeply unpopular relatives.

1530 > After a siege by the combined papal and imperial forces, Florence is obliged to receive Alessandro, who was proclaimed Duke of Florence, the first Medici to bear the title of ruler.

1537 > Alessandro is assassinated and power passes to another Cosimo (not a direct heir but rather a descendant of Cosimo il Vecchio's brother), thanks to support from the emperor Charles V, whose daughter was married to Alessandro.

1557 > Cosimo buys the territory of Siena from the Habsburgs, giving Florence control of all of Tuscany with the solitary exception of Lucca. Two years later Florentine hegemony in Tuscany is confirmed in the Treaty of Cateau-Cambrésis, the final act in the Wars of Italy.

1570 > Cosimo takes the title Cosimo I, Grand Duke of Tuscany. In European terms Tuscany is a second-rank power, but it's one of the strongest states in Italy. Cosimo builds the Uffizi, extends and overhauls the Palazzo Vecchio, installs the Medici in the Palazzo Pitti, has the Ponte Santa Trinita constructed across the Arno and commissions much of the public sculpture around the Piazza della Signoria. His descendants remain in power until 1737.

1630s > The market for Florence's woollen goods collapses, and the city's banks go into a terminal slump.

1737 > Under the terms of a treaty signed by Anna Maria de'

Medici (the sister of Gian Gastone de' Medici, the last male Medici) Florence passes to the House of Lorraine, cousins of the Austrian Habsburgs.

1799 > Napoleon dislodges the Austrians from Italy, but after his fall from power the Lorraine dynasty is brought back, remaining in residence until the last of the line, Leopold II, consents to his own deposition in 1859.

1865 > Florence becomes the capital of the new Kingdom of Italy, a position it holds until 1870, when Rome takes over. The city's subsequent decline is accelerated by the economic disruption that follows World War I.

1943 > After the Allied landing at Monte Cassino, Tuscany is a battlefield between the Nazis and the partisans. Substantial parts of Florence are wrecked by the retreating German army, who bomb all the bridges except the Ponte Vecchio and blow up much of the medieval city near the banks of the Arno.

Since World War II > After World War II the province of Florence establishes itself as the third largest industrial centre in Italy. Textiles, metalwork, glass, ceramics, pharmaceuticals and chemical production remain major industries in the province, while in Florence itself many long-established crafts continue to thrive, notably jewellery and gold-working, the manufacture of handmade paper, perfumery and leatherwork. But tourism is the mainstay of the Florentine economy, with the city attracting around eight million tourists a year.

Italian

What follows is a brief pronunciation guide and a run down of essential words and phrases. For more detail, get *Italian: Rough Guide Phrasebook*.

Pronunciation

Italian **pronunciation** is easy, since every word is spoken exactly as it is written. The only difficulties you are likely to encounter are the few consonants that are different from English:

c before e or i is pronounced as in **ch**urch, while **ch** before the same vowels is hard, as in **c**at.

sci or **sce** are pronounced as in **sh**eet and **sh**elter respectively.

g is soft before **e** and **i**, as in **g**eranium; hard when followed by **h**, as in **g**arlic.

gn has the ni sound of our "o**ni**on".

gl in Italian is softened to something like li in English, as in sta**lli**on.

h is not aspirated, as in **h**onour.

All Italian words are stressed on the penultimate syllable unless an accent (´ or `) denotes otherwise, although written accents are often left out in practice. Note that the ending -ia or -ie counts as two syllables, hence *trattoria* is stressed on the i.

Words and phrases

BASIC WORDS AND PHRASES

Good morning	Buon giorno
Good afternoon/ evening	Buona sera
Good night	Buona notte
Goodbye	Arrivederci
Yes	Sì
No	No
Please	Per favore
Thank you (very much)	Grázie (molte/ mille grazie)
You're welcome	Prego
Alright/that's OK	Va bene

How are you?	Come stai/sta? (informal/formal)
I'm fine	Bene
Do you speak English?	Parla inglese?
I don't understand	Non ho capito
I don't know	Non lo so
Excuse me	Mi scusi/Prego
Excuse me (in a crowd)	Permesso
I'm sorry	Mi dispiace
I'm English	Sono inglese
Scottish	scozzese
American	americano
Irish	irlandese
Welsh	gallese
Today	Oggi
Tomorrow	Domani
Day after tomorrow	Dopodomani
Yesterday	Ieri
Now	Adesso
Later	Più tardi
Wait a minute!	Aspetta!
In the morning	Di mattina
In the afternoon	Nel pomeriggio
In the evening	Di sera
Here/there	Qui/Là
Good/bad	Buono/Cattivo
Big/small	Grande/Piccoo
Cheap/expensive	Económico/Caro
Hot/cold	Caldo/Freddo
Near/far	Vicino/Lontano
Vacant/occupied	Libero/Occupato
With/without	Con/Senza
More/less	Più/Meno
Enough, no more	Basta
Mr...	Signor...
Mrs...	Signora...
Miss...	Signorina... (il Signor, la Signora, la Signorina when speaking about someone else)

NUMBERS

1	uno
2	due
3	tre
4	quattro

5	cinque
6	sei
7	sette
8	otto
9	nove
10	dieci
11	undici
12	dodici
13	tredici
14	quattordici
15	quindici
16	sedici
17	diciassette
18	diciotto
19	diciannove
20	venti
21	ventuno
22	ventidue
30	trenta
40	quaranta
50	cinquanta
60	sessanta
70	settanta
80	ottanta
90	novanta
100	cento
101	centuno
110	centodieci
200	duecento
500	cinquecento
1000	mille
5000	cinquemila
10,000	diecimila
50,000	cinquantamila

SOME SIGNS

Entrata/Uscita	Entrance/exit
Aperto/Chiuso	Open/closed
Arrivi/Partenze	Arrivals/departures
Chiuso per restauro	Closed for restoration
Chiuso per ferie	Closed for holidays
Tirare/Spingere	Pull/push
Non toccare	Do not touch
Perícolo	Danger
Attenzione	Beware
Pronto soccorso	First aid
Vietato fumare	No smoking

TRANSPORT

Traghetto	Ferry
Autostazione	Bus station
Stazione ferroviaria	Train station
Un biglietto a . . .	A ticket to . . .
Solo andata/andata e ritorno	One-way/return
A che ora parte?	What time does it leave?
Da dove parte?	Where does it leave from?

ACCOMMODATION

Albergo	Hotel
Ha una cámera...	Do you have a room...
per una/due/treperson(a/e)	for one/two/three people
per una/due/trenott(e/i)	for one/two/three nights
con un letto matrimoniale	with a double bed
con una doccia/un bagno	with a shower/bath
Quanto costa?	How much is it?
È compresa la prima colazione?	Is breakfast included?
Ha niente che costa di meno?	Do you have anything cheaper?
La prendo	I'll take it
Vorrei prenotare una cámera	I'd like to book a room
Ho una prenotazione	I have a booking
Ostello per la gioventù	Youth hostel

IN THE RESTAURANT

Una tavola	A table
Vorrei prenotare una tavola per due alle otto	I'd like to book a table for two people at eight o'clock
Abbiamo bisogno di un coltello	We need a knife
una forchetta	a fork
un cucchiaio	a spoon
un bicchiere	a glass
Che cosa mi consiglia lei?	What do you recommend?
Cameriere/a!	Waiter/waitress!
Il conto	Bill/check

| È incluso il servizio? | Is service included? |
| Sono vegetariano/a | I'm a vegetarian |

QUESTIONS AND DIRECTIONS

Dove?	Where?
(Dov'è/Dove sono)?	(where is/are ...?)
Quando?	When?
Cosa? (Cos'è?)	What? (what is it?)
Quanto/Quanti?	How much/many?
Perché?	Why?
È/C'è È/C'è ...?)	It is/there is
	(is it/is there...?)
Che ora è/	What time is it?
Che ore sono?	
Come arrivo a...?	How do I get to...?
A che ora apre?	What time does
	it open?
A che ora chiude?	What time does
	it close?
Quanto costa?	How much does it
(Quanto cóstano?)	cost ?
	(...do they cost?)
Come si chiama in	What's it called in
italiano?	Italian?

Menu reader
BASICS AND SNACKS

Aceto	Vinegar
Aglio	Garlic
Biscotti	Biscuits
Burro	Butter
Caramelle	Sweets
Cioccolato	Chocolate
Focaccia	Oven-baked bread-based snack
Formaggio	Cheese
Frittata	Omelette
Gelato	Ice cream
Grissini	Bread sticks
Marmellata	Jam
Olio	Oil
Olive	Olives
Pane	Bread
Pane integrale	Wholemeal bread
Panino	Bread roll
Patatine	Crisps
Patatine fritte	Chips
Pepe	Pepper
Pizzetta	Small cheese and tomato pizza
Riso	Rice

Sale	Salt
Tramezzini	Sandwich
Uova	Eggs
Yogurt	Yoghurt
Zucchero	Sugar
Zuppa	Soup

STARTERS (ANTIPASTI)

Antipasto misto	Mixed cold meats and cheese (and a selection of other things in this list)
Caponata	Mixed aubergine, olives, tomatoes and celery
Caprese	Tomato and mozzarella salad
Crostini di milza	Minced spleen on pieces of toast
Donzele/donzelline	Fried dough balls
Fettuna/ bruschetta	Garlic toast with olive oil
Finocchiona	Pork sausage flavoured with fennel
Insalata di mare	Seafood salad
Insalata di riso	Rice salad
Melanzane in parmigiana	Fried aubergine in tomato and parmesan cheese
Mortadella	Salami-type cured meat
Pancetta	Bacon
Peperonata	Grilled green, red or yellow peppers stewed in olive oil
Pinzimonio	Raw seasonal vegetable in olive oil, with salt and pepper
Pomodori ripieni	Stuffed tomatoes
Prosciutto	Ham
Prosciutto di cinghiale	Cured wild boar ham
Salame	Salami
Salame toscano	Pork sausage with pepper and cubes of fat
Salsicce	Pork or wild boar sausage

THE FIRST COURSE (IL PRIMO)

SOUPS

Acquacotta	Onion soup served with toast and poached egg
Brodo	Clear broth
Cacciucco	Fish stew with tomatoes, bread and red wine
Carabaccia	Onion soup
Garmugia	Soup made with fava beans, peas, artichokes, asparagus and bacon
Minestra di farro	Wheat and bean soup
Minestrina	Any light soup
Minestrone	Thick vegetable soup
Minestrone alla fiorentina	Haricot bean soup with red cabbage, tomatoes, onions and herbs
Panzanella	Summer salad of tomatoes, basil, cucumber, onion and bread
Pappa al pomodoro	Tomato soup thickened with bread
Pasta e fagioli	Pasta soup with beans
Pastina in brodo	Pasta pieces in clear broth
Ribollita	Winter vegetable soup, based on beans and thickened with bread
Stracciatella	Broth with egg
Zuppa di fagioli	Bean soup

PASTA AND GNOCCHI

Cannelloni	Large tubes of pasta, stuffed
Farfalle	Literally "bow"-shaped pasta; the word also means "butterflies"
Fettuccine	Narrow pasta ribbons
Gnocchi	Small potato and dough dumplings
Gnocchi di ricotta	Dumplings filled with ricotta and spinach
Lasagne	Lasagne
Maccheroni	Tubular spaghetti
Pappardelle (con lepre)	Wide, short noodles, often served with hare sauce
Pasta al forno	Pasta baked with minced meat, eggs, tomato and cheese
Pasta alla carrettiera	Pasta with tomato, garlic, pepper, parsley and chilli
Penne	Smaller version of rigatoni
Penne strasciate	Quill-shaped pasta in meat sauce
Ravioli	Small packets of stuffed pasta
Rigatoni	Large, grooved, tubular pasta
Risotto	Cooked rice dish, with sauce
Spaghetti	Spaghetti
Spaghettini	Thin spaghetti
Tagliatelle	Pasta ribbons; another word for fettucine
Tortellini	Small rings of pasta, stuffed with meat or cheese
Vermicelli	Very thin spaghetti (literally "little worms")

PASTA SAUCES

Aglio e olio (e peperoncino)	Tossed in garlic and olive oil (and hot chillies)
Arrabiata	Spicy tomato sauce
Bolognese	Meat sauce
Burro e salvia	Butter and sage
Carbonara	Cream, ham and beaten egg
Frutta di mare	Seafood
Funghi	Mushroom
Matriciana	Cubed pork and tomato sauce
Panna	Cream

Parmigiano	Parmesan cheese
Pesto	Ground basil, pine nut, garlic and pecorino sauce
Pomodoro	Tomato sauce
Ragù	Meat sauce
Vóngole	Clam and tomato sauce

THE SECOND COURSE (IL SECONDO)

MEAT (CARNE)

Agnello	Lamb
Arista	Roast pork loin with garlic and rosemary
Bistecca	Steak
Bistecca alla fiorentina	Thick grilled T-bone steak
Cibreo	Chicken liver and egg stew
Coniglio	Rabbit
Costolette	Chops
Cotolette	Cutlets
Fegatini	Chicken livers
Fégato	Liver
Involtini	Steak slices, rolled and stuffed
Lingua	Tongue
Lombatina	Veal chop
Maiale	Pork
Manzo	Beef
Ossobuco	Shin of veal
Peposo	Peppered beef stew
Pollo	Chicken
Pollo alla diavola/ al mattone	Chicken flattened with a brick, grilled with herbs
Polpette	Meatballs (or minced balls of anything)
Rognoni	Kidneys
Salsiccia	Sausage
Saltimbocca	Veal with ham
Scottiglia	Stew of veal, game and poultry, cooked with white wine and tomatoes
Spezzatino	Stew

Spiedini di maiale	Skewered spiced cubes of pork loin and liver, with bread and bay leaves
Tacchino	Turkey
Trippa	Tripe
Trippa alla fiorentina	Tripe in tomato sauce, served with parmesan
Vitello	Veal

FISH (PESCE) AND SHELLFISH (CROSTACEI)

Acciughe	Anchovies
Anguilla	Eel
Aragosta	Lobster
Baccalà alla livornese	Salt cod with garlic, tomatoes and parsley
Bronzino/Branzino	Sea bass
Calamari	Squid
Caparossoli	Shrimps
Cape sante	Scallops
Coda di rospo	Monkfish
Cozze	Mussels
Dentice	Dentex (like sea bass)
Gamberetti	Shrimps
Gámberi	Prawns
Granchio	Crab
Orata	Bream
Ostriche	Oysters
Pescespada	Swordfish
Polpo	Octopus
Rombo	Turbot
San Pietro	John Dory
Sarde	Sardines
Schie	Shrimps
Seppie	Cuttlefish
Sógliola	Sole
Tonno	Tuna
Tonno con fagioli	Tuna with white beans and raw onion
Triglie	Red mullet
Trota	Trout
Vóngole	Clams

VEGETABLES (CONTORNI) AND SALAD (INSALATA)

| Asparagi | Asparagus |

Asparagi alla fiorentina	Asparagus with butter, fried egg and cheese
Basílico	Basil
Bróccoli	Broccoli
Cápperi	Capers
Carciofi	Artichokes
Carciofini	Artichoke hearts
Carotte	Carrots
Cavolfiori	Cauliflower
Cávolo	Cabbage
Ceci	Chickpeas
Cetriolo	Cucumber
Cipolla	Onion
Fagioli	Beans
Fagioli all'uccelletto	White beans cooked with tomatoes, garlic and sage
Fagiolini	Green beans
Finocchio	Fennel
Frittata di carciofi	Fried artichoke flan
Funghi	Mushrooms
Insalata verde/ insalata mista	Green salad/ mixed salad
Melanzana	Aubergine/eggplant
Patate	Potatoes
Peperoni	Peppers
Piselli	Peas
Pomodori	Tomatoes
Radicchio	Chicory
Spinaci	Spinach
Zucca	Pumpkin
Zucchini	Courgettes

DESSERTS (DOLCI)

Amaretti	Macaroons
Brigidini	Anise wafer biscuits
Buccellato	Anise raisin cake
Cantucci/cantuccini	Small almond biscuits, served with Vinsanto wine
Cassata	Ice cream cake with candied fruit
Castagnaccio	Unleavened chestnut-flour cake containing raisins, walnuts and rosemary
Cenci	Fried dough dusted with powdered sugar
Frittelle di riso	Rice fritters
Gelato	Ice cream
Macedonia	Fruit salad
Meringa	Frozen meringue with whipped cream and chocolate
Necci	Chestnut-flour crêpes
Panforte	Hard fruit, nut and spice cake
Ricciarelli	Marzipan almond biscuits
Schiacciata alla fiorentina	Orange-flavoured cake covered with powdered sugar, eaten at carnival time
Schiacciata con l'uva	Grape- and sugar-covered bread dessert
Torta	Cake, tart
Zabaglione	Dessert made with eggs, sugar and Marsala wine
Zuccotto	Sponge cake filled with chocolate and whipped cream
Zuppa Inglese	Trifle

CHEESE (FORMAGGI)

Caciocavallo	A type of dried, mature mozzarella cheese
Fontina	Northern Italian cheese used in cooking
Gorgonzola	Soft blue-veined cheese
Mozzarella	Bland, soft white cheese used on pizzas
Parmigiano	Parmesan
Pecorino	Strong-tasting hard sheep's cheese
Provolone	Hard strong cheese
Ricotta	Soft white cheese made from ewe's

milk, used in sweet or savoury dishes

FRUIT AND NUTS (FRUTTA AND NOCE)

Ananas	Pineapple
Arance	Oranges
Banane	Bananas
Ciliegie	Cherries
Fichi	Figs
Frágole	Strawberries
Limone	Lemon
Mándorle	Almonds
Mele	Apples
Melone	Melon
Pere	Pears
Pesche	Peaches
Pignoli	Pine nuts
Pistacchio	Pistachio nut
Uve	Grapes

COOKING TERMS

Affumicato	Smoked
Al dente	Firm, not overcooked
Al ferro	Grilled without oil
Al forno	Baked
Al Marsala	Cooked with Marsala wine
Al vapore	Steamed
Alla brace	Barbecued
Alla griglia	Grilled
Allo spiedo	On the spit
Arrosto	Roasted
Ben cotto	Well done
Bollito	Boiled
Brasato	Cooked in wine
Cotto	Cooked (not raw)
Crudo	Raw
Fritto	Fried

In úmido	Stewed
Lesso	Boiled
Milanese	Fried in egg and breadcrumbs
Pizzaiola	Cooked with tomato sauce
Ripieno	Stuffed
Sangue	Rare
Surgelato	Frozen

DRINKS

Acqua minerale	Mineral water
Alla spina	Draught (beer)
Aranciata	Orangeade
Bicchiere	Glass
Birra	Beer
Bottiglia	Bottle
Caffè	Coffee
Cioccolata calda	Hot chocolate
Ghiaccio	Ice
Granita	Iced coffee or fruit drink
Latte	Milk
Limonata	Lemonade
Selz	Soda water
Spremuta	Fresh fruit juice
Spumante	Sparkling wine
Succo	Concentrated fruit juice with sugar
Tè	Tea
Tónico	Tonic water
Vino	Wine
Rosso	Red
Bianco	White
Rosato	Rosé
Secco	Dry
Dolce	Sweet
Litro	Litre
Mezzo	Half
Quarto	Quarter
Salute!	Cheers!

PUBLISHING INFORMATION

This first edition published March 2014 by **Rough Guides Ltd**

80 Strand, London WC2R 0RL

11, Community Centre, Panchsheel Park, New Delhi 110017, India

Distributed by the Penguin Group

Penguin Books Ltd, 80 Strand, London WC2R 0RL

Penguin Group (USA) 345 Hudson Street, NY 10014, USA

Penguin Group (Australia) 250 Camberwell Road, Camberwell, Victoria 3124, Australia

Penguin Group (NZ) 67 Apollo Drive, Mairangi Bay, Auckland 1310, New Zealand

Penguin Group (South Africa) Block D, Rosebank Office Park, 181 Jan Smuts Avenue, Parktown North, Gauteng, South Africa 2193

Rough Guides is represented in Canada by

Tourmaline Editions Inc., 662 King Street West, Suite 304, Toronto, Ontario, M5V 1M7

Typeset in Minion and Din to an original design by Henry Iles and Dan May.

Printed and bound in China

© Rough Guides 2014

Maps © Rough Guides

No part of this book may be reproduced in any form without permission from the publisher except for the quotation of brief passages in reviews.

168pp includes index

A catalogue record for this book is available from the British Library

ISBN 978-1-40933-033-2

The publishers and authors have done their best to ensure the accuracy and currency of all the information in **Pocket Rough Guide Florence**, however, they can accept no responsibility for any loss, injury, or inconvenience sustained by any traveller as a result of information or advice contained in the guide.

1 3 5 7 9 8 6 4 2

MIX
Paper from
responsible sources
FSC™ C018179
www.fsc.org

ROUGH GUIDES CREDITS

Text editor: Lucy Kane

Layout: Pradeep Thapliyal

Cartography: Katie Bennett

Picture editor: Wilf Matos

Photographer: Diana Jarvis

Production: Linda Dare

Proofreader: Diane Margolis

Managing editor: Monica Woods

Cover design: Wilf Matos, Dan May and Pradeep Thapliyal

THE AUTHOR

Jonathan Buckley (🌐 jonathan-buckley.co.uk) has written and contributed to several Rough Guides, and is an Advisory Fellow of the Royal Literary Fund. He has published eight novels.

ACKNOWLEDGEMENTS

Jonathan Buckley would like to thank Lucy Kane and Wilf Matos for making the editorial process as smooth as possible.

HELP US UPDATE

We've gone to a lot of effort to ensure that the first edition of the **Pocket Rough Guide Florence** is accurate and up-to-date. However, things change – places get "discovered", opening hours are notoriously fickle, restaurants and rooms raise prices or lower standards. If you feel we've got it wrong or left something out, we'd like to know, and if you can remember the address, the price, the hours, the phone number, so much the better.

Please send your comments with the subject line "**Pocket Rough Guide Florence Update**" to ✉ mail@roughguides.com. We'll credit all contributions and send a copy of the next edition (or any other Rough Guide if you prefer) for the very best emails.

Find more travel information, connect with fellow travellers and book your trip on ⓦ roughguides.com

PHOTO CREDITS

All images © Rough Guides except the following:
(Key: a-above; b-below/bottom; c-centre; f-far; l-left; r-right; t-top)

Front cover Getty Images/Danita Delimont
Back cover Corbis/Jeremy Woodhouse
Inside front cover Getty Images/ Gamma-Rapho (t); Superstock/Travel Library Ltd (c)

p.1 Corbis/Sylvain Sonnet
p.4 Corbis/Sylvain Sonnet
p.5 AWL Images/Peter Adams
p.6 Corbis/Guido Cozzi
p.8 Corbis/Roger de la Harpe (t)
p.9 Corbis/Sandro Vannini (t)
p.11 SuperStock/Cubo Images (br)
p.12 Corbis/Sylvain Sonnet
p.15 Corbis/Sylvain Sonnet (cr, cl, b)
p.16 SuperStock/Hemis.fr

p.17 SuperStock/Jose Antonio Moreno/age fotostock (t); Alamy/David South (b)
p.18 SuperStock/DeAgostini
p.23 Ora d'Aria (t)
p.27 Getty Images/DeAgostini (t); SuperStock/ Photoservice Electa/Universal Images Group (br)
p.37 SuperStock: Photoservice Electa/ Universal Images Group
p.38 Corbis/Sylvain Sonnet
p.43 Getty Images/Dea Picture Library
p.47 Corbis/Luigi Casentini
p.58 Corbis/Ken Kaminesky
p.92 Corbis/Sylvain Sonnet
p.132 Royal Demeure Hotels, *Helvetia & Bristol*/Andrea Getuli and Giovanni Rinaldi
p.142 SuperStock/Tips Images

Index

Maps are marked in **bold**.

INDEX

MAKE THE MOST
OF YOUR GADGETS

roughguides.com/downloads

FROM **ANDROID** TO **iPADS** TO **SOCIAL MEDIA**

BOOKS | EBOOKS | APPS

www.roughguides.com
MAKE THE MOST OF YOUR TIME ON EARTH